D0531596

OVERLOOKED CHRISTIANITY

OVERLOOKED CHRISTIANITY

by
Gene
Edwards

4

Overlooked Christianity
Copyright 1997 by Gene Edwards
Published by The SeedSowers
            P.O.Box 285, Sargent, GA 30275

Library of Congress Cataloging-in-Publication Data

Edwards, Gene, 1932 -
        Overlooked Christianity / Gene Edwards
        ISBN 0-940-232-588
        1. Spiritual Life. 1. Title
        Catalog Card Number:

Printed in the United States of America

Times New Roman 12pt

Dedication

I take this opportunity to name some of the men who have influenced my life.

Harvey Lewis
Pastor of the First Baptist Church in my home town of Cleveland, Texas at the time of my conversion.

E.R.Page
Pastor of the First Baptist Church in Commerce, Texas, where I was a university student at the time of my conversion.

Daws Trotman
Founder of the Navigators who was gracious enough to spend the greater part of a day with a nineteen year old.

Dr Crabtree
Professor of Theology - International Baptist Seminary in Ruschlikon, Switzerland

Bill Bright
Founder of Campus Crusade for Christ

Ray Summers
Jack McGorman
Cal Guy
Professors at Southwestern Baptist Theological Seminary

Acknowledgement

I want to express my appreciation
to Jerry Coulter, who labored hard to bring the
audio tapes and manuscript of this book
into workable form.

I also want to express my appreciation
to Jenny Jeffries, who had the gargantuous task
of reworking draft after draft of this book.

Author's Preface

The basic content of this manuscript came into being during a period of time, when I was twenty-nine, in which I had taken a year off from the ministry to seek out for my own heart's sake, an understanding of what really happened in the first century.

I did not do this, as so many have, by taking one verse here and another verse there and putting together some doctrine or teaching. Contrariwise, I let the story tell itself in a forward moving, unbroken chronological order. What emerged was a look at the practical side of God on deeply spiritual matters.

My life was forever changed.

Seven years later I brought a message on this subject which was called "Foundation Stones." A few years after that, I brought a series on it, and kept the title "Foundation Stones." These messages would probably have remained untouched for the rest of my life, except for the efforts of Jerry Coulter, author of *Beholding and Becoming*. He worked long and hard bringing these messages into coherence.

It was because of Jerry's efforts that I decided I would publish this book; but, once I lent myself to the task, I found there was much and formidable work to be done. With the possible exception of *The Divine Romance*, I have labored over this book more than any other work; yet you will not find in it the sublime element of *A Tale of Three Kings*, *Prisoner in the Third Cell*, or most of the other books which I have put out.

The content of this book, the depth of this book, the revelation from which this book comes, have eluded even the author! This book will always be inadequate because the revelation of Christ and His way is always beyond men's capacity to embrace. Despite that fact, some day in the future this book may be found to be one of the most important books I will have ever written.*

There will not be many people who will read this book, but among that small group, there will be those who will find that what is written on these pages deals with ultimate issues.

I commend this book to every believer; and to every believer who reads this book, I would ask you to put it in the hands of Christian workers.

If this book lacks merit, charge that to my inadequacies and feeble efforts. If it strikes fire, then be assured *that* is because Jesus Christ has revealed to you some of the secrets of His ways.

I have requested the publisher make only one printing of this book as I know its audience will be small in number. Nonetheless, it may prove to be one of the most important books that I pen.

Choosing a title for this book has been the most difficult part of writing it. (I am open to suggestion in case this book is ever reissued post-humously.)

May this book fall into the hands of hot-headed young men and women who do not fit into and cannot abide the present-day practice of the Christian faith.

If you discover such a person, may you be the one who puts this book in his hands.

A companion volume is planned. It will deal with the way Jesus Christ and Paul of Tarsus raised up workers.

The books Revolution, The Silas Diary, and the other books in that series (which are on the subject of what really happened in the first century) I think of as just one book. Those volumes, consisting of one story, would also fall into the category of being one of the most important books I shall ever pen.

1

The year was 18 A.D.

The place was Nazareth.

Three young men in Nazareth all reached twenty-one years of age, and all decided what to do with their lives. Two of these men made a choice identical to the choice we evangelical Christians make.

Their decision was wrong. So is ours. Perfectly acceptable decisions. Human decisions. Logical decisions. Christian decisions, you might say. But still wrong.

The third young man made a divine decision.

Their names were Mathias, Zephan and Jesus.

Mathias packed his belongings one morning and said good-bye to his friend Jesus, then struck out for Jerusalem, rented a room near the temple and began, at age twenty-one, to study to be a *scribe.* His training was virtually identical to the way you and I prepare to be ministers, but it was and is still *man's way of doing things.*

God's way of raising up workers is not like

this. His way may be lost to us, but it still remains God's way of doing things.

Go to Jerusalem, sit under teachers for nine years: Is this really a good idea? It's the way we do it, but it is wrong. This approach to training men kills the faith. We desperately need to stop this way of training men called of God. At least some of us must.

It is not just the wrong way; it is also dangerous.

Some twelve years after Mathias left Nazareth and moved to Jerusalem, he helped to crucify Jesus Christ.

And Zephan? Zephan also packed his sack, bade his friend Jesus good-bye and he set out for Jerusalem for nine years of training to become a *priest*. This training was also wrong. Twelve years later he also helped to crucify Jesus.

These two men were trained in ways *too* similar to the way we train men today. . .Bible schools and seminaries.

Even forgetting seminaries and Bible schools and the way those traditional institutions raise up workers, let's look at the most revolutionary things going on in today's Christianity, the way of the radical, creative, imaginative. . .*house church movement*.

Let's meet Matt and Pat, who are modern counterparts to Mathias and Zephan.

Matt is called of God. He has raised up a house church. Listen to him. Every other sentence he utters is peppered with phrases like "Know the Bible" and "Be careful, many false teachers are out there who don't believe the Bible is the Word of God," and "The Bible teaches about church discipline."

Sounds good! Here is a young man obedient to God's Word . . .or at least let's hope that's what he is obeying. What of the people Matt ministers to in that living room? Matt gives his people all sorts of teachings. Picking a verse here and a verse there, he tells everyone what an apostle, an elder, and a deacon are, "as taught in the pure Word of God." Matt will soon have elders and deacons in his home church—and they will come into being, based on "what the Bible teaches about these things."

Matt knows the Bible incredibly well, but there is a flaw. Matt knows what he has been taught. (He was never in a house church until he started this one; he started it on theory.) But there is an even greater flaw. Matt does not know Jesus Christ very well. He is also teaching facts. . .information. . . and more information. . .but he has little personal experience which is *encounter*.

Matt was trained well, by today's standard of how we do things, but Matt knows almost nothing of significant value about how to live the Christian life or how to experience Christ. Nor does he know much that is imbedded in reality which has to do with the life of the ecclesia. . .*first-century style*. He also didn't become a worker by first-century means—not by God's way of doing things.

Jesus Christ has a way. A way to *raise up* workers. A way to *learn* to live the Christian life. A way to *raise up* the church. And a way for there *to be* church life. . .first-century style.

Matt is so committed to the Bible, or at least to the way he was taught to see the Bible, that he cannot really believe he is dysfunctional. For Matt, commitment to, teaching of, and knowledge of the New Testament take the place of knowing Christ experientially and knowing a living experience of Christ and of church life.

Matt might get angry if you tell him this. Matt's reply will be to quote the Scripture in order to defend his methodology. (This is not God's way of doing things.)

Matt knows his Bible, twenty-*first* century style. But he

just might, in circumstances similar to Matthias', crucify Jesus Christ.

Could this be true?

If he met Jesus, and Jesus was not approaching Scripture in the way Matt does, and if Jesus was a threat to the Bible (a la Matt's view), he just might not step in to prevent the crucifying. Matt would defend his position as being "in defense of the Word of God."

There is a problem in doing things man's way: We really believe it is God's way.

Dear reader, there is an evangelical Christian mind-set. It is a mind-set which needs to be shattered. One aspect of that mind-set is the way of training Christian workers. It is not God's way. In addition, our mind-set on the way churches are started and the way we "practice church" are not God's way either. Our way of showing God's people how to have a daily, living relationship to Christ is also the wrong way. Our "how to live the Christian life" is askew. Again, this evangelical mind-set needs to be broken.

This book is about finding again God's way of doing these very things.

Now let's move on to Pat. Pat is the counterpart of Zephan. He is totally *clergy centered.*

Pat is also starting a house church. He sees himself as a radical. He will never admit it, but despite all he preaches and all his convictions, he will end up being pastor of the house church he started. How so?

Pat will always be the center—all will look to him. Pat has the answers, or at least that is the general impression of his people. Pat is a modern-day version of a priest. As with all priests, God's people (in this case, the ecclesia meeting in a home) will forever depend on Pat. Wrap it in any kind or shape of box, color it any color, use any vocabulary you wish, but it still comes out sacerdotalism.

Pat has been ministering for four years, after having been in a seminary for three years. None of the training nor the ministry looks much like Jesus' ten years of training that He received in a carpenter's shop or His four years of ministry. Pat's way of doing things doesn't look much like Paul's way of raising up churches or training workers either.

There are many things wrong about Pat's training and his ministry. One thing is this—Pat doesn't act like the rest of us, nor dress like us, nor talk like us. A rose by any other name is still a rose. A priest by any other name, even without the costume, is still a priest.

But there is something in Pat more insidious and subtle. Pat will never see the ecclesia. . .that is, he cannot grasp the living entity of ecclesia (i.e., church life). He sees ministry—*first* and foremost. He has a *clergy* reference, a *ministry* reference. The church, for Pat and all the sons of Pat, is but an *instrument of ministry*. God's people are naught but an instrument of ministry. The church of God is but a means to an end, for the minister.

You doubt?

Pat will never let go of ministry. He will minister to those house churches forever. They will listen. Forever, ministry. . . forever listening. . .forever! More tragic still, the people listening will forever have a *minister* reference too. They will *never* even be able to conceptualize that a minister can *depart* the church and leave the church totally in the hands of laymen. Pat will never know what it means to be *sent*; the people of God who sit under him will never know what it means to be *left*. Neither Pat nor his people will ever see or experience *church life*; yet such experience is God's way.

This mind-set, this evangelical mind-set of the eternally talking tongue and the eternally listening ear *must* end.

God's way of doing things? It is for you and for me as Christians to *first* experience church life. If you are a worker, you become a worker *after* being in ecclesia life.

Should you attempt to minister—having never known church life—then even if you *talk about* church life, you will never *bring forth church life*. Not in your own life, not in other lives.

Church life is not a *thing*. *She* is a living organism. You *encounter* her, you grow up in her.

Jesus Christ experienced church life first, then He ministered. So also with all the other Christian workers of the first century. This part is overlooked!

Conversion, Christ-centeredness, experience of church life, then (and only then) ministry. That's God's way of doing things.

What we have seen in this chapter is that Pat was trained in a wrong way to be a Christian worker. Further, like Mathias, Matt and Pat know little about *how to live the Christian life*. This, too, is unbelievably overlooked. *How to deeply know and experience Jesus Christ* is not really engraved in Matt or Pat. Further, Pat has no long-term exposure to, nor experiential knowledge of, the *ecclesia*. Neither Matt nor Pat are properly trained, nor have they any idea of the way Jesus or Paul did things.

Pat is great at preaching, great at prophecy, and even greater at discerning the problems of Christendom. Such experience, training and giftedness. . .though accepted as the norm. . .nonetheless are worthless in dealing with *realms unseen*.

May your generation rediscover God's ancient eternal ways!

In the pages to follow, we will look in more detail at all the matters about which you have just read; and, as we follow the New Testament story, we will refer back to these very issues and see them from several vantage points.

Now let us return to Nazareth.

2

There is still one of the three young men who is twenty-one years old who has not yet left town. His name is Jesus. Jesus was raised up *God's way*.

God's way of doing things is best seen in the way God raised up Jesus.

How did God go about showing His Son Jesus how to live the Christian life? How did God go about showing His Son church life? How did God train His Son to be a Christian worker? In these you see *God's* way of doing things.

The way God does things in these areas is what this book is about.

Yes, God's way of doing these things has disappeared from the faith. But that doesn't mean they can't be rediscovered. Overlooked does *not* mean *lost* forever.

There are many men today who want to serve God. They will probably be trained Matt and Mathias' way. Or Zephan and Pat's way. But God's way is still possible.

Just how was Jesus prepared for the ministry?

He is twenty-one. One morning he, too, like Mathias and Zephan, walks out of his house, bids his mother good-bye and goes, not to Jerusalem to study, but to a *carpenter shop*. Jesus Christ becomes a blue-collar worker—chisel, saw, splinters in hands, sunburned, in a workshop. Those were the surroundings of *His* training.

Dear church worker, take note. Is this the divine way? Is this the first hint of God's way of doing things?

God's way to train someone
    to be a Christian
        to learn to live the Christian life
        to know church life
            to be a Christian worker
            and to train others

Is there a distinct pattern to His way of doing these things? One that is contrary to our evangelical ways? One that has been overlooked?

Return with me to. . .well. . .eternity past! That's where God's way of doing things had its *first* beginning. In eternity past, the Father taught His Son how to live the Christian life, He taught Him how to be a Christian worker, and He even taught His Son. . .church life!!

Later, God did all this all over again in *space-time*. In Nazareth of Galilee, this twenty-one-year-old Jesus continued (for the *second* time) to receive training from His Father. It was a way of being trained that was identical to the way God had trained Him in *eternity*.

*   *   *

Jesus the Christ had lived the Christian life as the Son of God in the eternals. He learned how to do this from the Father.

Jesus the Carpenter learned, as a man, how to live the Christian life on the earth. . .also from the Father.

In Galilee, He lived church life in His fellowship with the Father and the Holy Spirit *in eternity.*

In Nazareth, Jesus Christ the Carpenter experienced church life with the Father and the Holy Spirit here on earth again. Later it was church life experienced by not three, but by thirteen. . .here on earth. Yes, twelve men were trained by Jesus Christ in the way God raised up Jesus!

Jesus the Christ trained in eternity.

Jesus the Christ continued to be trained in how to be a Christian worker on earth, in the same way He had been trained in eternity.

Jesus the Christ trained twelve men. How? By the same means His Father had trained Him.

* * *

When Jesus finally began His ministry, He demonstrated to twelve men His internal fellowship with the Father. That is:

(1) He showed twelve men how to *live the Christian life* the way He Himself lived the Christian life.

(2) He showed twelve men church life.

(3) Every day the Lord showed twelve men how to be Christian workers *and* how to *train future Christian workers.*

The Son lived in the presence of God. The twelve lived in the presence of Jesus. In so doing they learned, in the very way the Son had learned. Twelve learned what a Christian worker is and how to be a Christian worker—by beholding Jesus, just as Jesus had beheld the Father.

This is God's way of doing things.

The Lord's way was His Father's way. . .the way the Father had worked these elements into the very nature and being of His Son.

Would you dare enter this ancient lineage?

3

There were Christians *before* creation, three of them!

Who were these first Christians? How did these three Christians live the Christian life? Learn *that*, and it will revolutionize your life. What resources were there for these *first* Christians to draw upon, in order to live the Christian life?

Were there practical tools? Or secrets? Or methods?

What, for them, were the bare essentials *necessary* for living the Christian life?

Now make a note of this principle: the principle of being there *from the beginning*. It is a principle which will hold throughout all the work of God.

Those *three* who were Christians, who were there *from the beginning*, what can they teach us about primordial ingredients of God's ways?

We are looking for the first motion. *Epistemology*, a look at first motions. That brings us to the very first Christian!

The First Christian

The Christian life was being lived by someone before creation. Preceding all physical matter was the Christian life. Preceding creation, there was already established *the way* to live the Christian life. That Christian life was lived out long before space-time and—mark this well—that Christian life was being lived *outside* of time and space.

The Christian life was (and is) always outside of space-time! The secret, the experience, the way, the source of living the Christian life is always outside the physical realm. The out-living of the Christian life always finds its resources in realms unseen—in realms free of all space-time continuums.

Who started all this? Just who was the first Christian?

The first Christian was the eternal Father. Though He doesn't predate the Son, nonetheless *all things* flow from the Father.

The Son, indeed, lived the Christian life in the bosom, in the very center and core, of God the Father. Jesus the Christ drew everything from the Father.

The Christian life is a very ancient thing! The Christian life and the *way* of living the Christian life preceded angels and even the heavenlies. As long as there has been the Trinity, there has been someone living the Christian life. (And there never was when there was no Trinity!) So, yes, the Christian life has been around a very long time.

And the living of it has a pattern, a *God's Way of doing things*.

That brings us to a fresh, new question. It is a question so exciting, the very asking of it is revolutionary.

How did the eternal Son of God live the Christian life? If ever there was an epistemological question, this is it! If ever there was a central question, this is it. If ever we are to know the "*how*" of living the Christian life, this is the first question to ask.

Just exactly how did the eternal Son live the Christian life?

Well, though we may not have been listening all that well, the Lord Jesus told us a great deal about the relationship He had with His Father *before* creation. During the thirty-three-year visitation of this planet, your Lord told us how He lived the Christian life way back then. That's not all. Again, we weren't listening all that carefully, but the Lord Jesus even showed us the *how*. What He demonstrated to us while here on earth was based on His past practice! Practical practice! Practical practice which He engaged in long before He created! Jesus showed us the pattern. He showed us God's way of living the Christian life.

The Lord told us, and then showed us, how the Christian life had been lived out in its most primitive practice. In its simplest practice. He revealed to us the *primordial* state of the Christian life. Herein lies *the secret* of living the Christian life. . .as known and experienced by no other than the *eternal* Son, *in* the Godhead, *before* creation.

How?

The Son of God lived the Christian life (in eternity past and later in Galilee):

> by an indwelling Father
> by the Father imparting His life to His Son
> by the Son living by means of the Father's life
> by the Son listening to His Father
> by the Son responding to what He heard the Father say
> by the Father revealing Himself to His Son

by the Son beholding His Father

by the Father loving the Son

by the Son loving the Father back with that very love
which the Father poured out on the Son

And, finally:

Take all of those elements together and you have the one secret, the only secret, the *only* pattern of the *how* of the Christian life. What you see in all of this is *the Son fellowshipping with the Father.*

Put it another way. All of the above, when combined, is the fellowship of the Godhead. That is how someone is supposed to live the Christian life! That is how all of us are supposed to live the Christian life! Anyone out there up to returning to *first* things? Things that were there *at the* beginning?

Dear reader, what went on in the Godhead constituted the beginning of a primitive, primordial pattern which God will *never* change.

Behold the first Christian! and the second! and the third! What you see here is how *they* lived out the secret of *how to live the Christian life.* Note that in *God's way* there are two primary elements in the life of the preincarnate Son:

(1) The Son draws life from His Father

(2) The Son fellowships with His Father.

This is the Christian life in its most primordial and primitive state. And it is *workable*! This is how the first Christians lived the Christian life and how *you* are meant to live the Christian life.

Did anyone ever tell you that? That *way* blows the soot out of all our concepts about how to live the Christian life. And if you do not yet grasp that fact, then look at all the things the eternal Son did *not* do in order to live the Christian life.

He did not tithe; He did not go to a Christian university; He did not speak in tongues; He did not read three chapters of His New Testament every day or pray twenty minutes before going to His carpenter's shop. The list of what He did *not* do is almost endless. Behold the irreducible minimum necessary to living the Christian life! But what of us? We must add to this list, right? We need more than this?

The answer is obvious: Yes, of course; after all, we are not the eternal Son of God, living there in the bosom of the Father before creation. On the other hand, that raises another question which demands an answer. Did the living out of the Christian life change once it made its way into creation? Did the way of the Christian life change when it entered space and time?

If the answer is yes, we will go on with living the Christian life as the evangelical mind-set presently prescribes for us. (Not a very appealing thought!) But if the outliving of the Christian life did not change, not so much as an iota, then we are on the threshold of a pragmatic revolution of our faith— and spiritual matters are about to undergo a cataclysmic change. Of course, we could deliberately decide *not* to live the Christian life the way the Son of God did! After all, we do get very attached to old ways and old wine. Failure can become addictive!

With all that said, let us look at a few other mind bogglers.

For instance; how did the Father tutor the Son in "living the Christian life"?

4

The primordial stage of the Christian life has been overlooked for seventeen hundred years.

The evangelical mind-set knows nothing of this pre-creation era.

Let's take a closer look at this age before creation. . .this crucial but overlooked part of Christianity.

Just how did the Father tutor the "other" Christian? The answer isn't the usual thing you hear. Here is the most overlooked of all things we have overlooked.

Apocalyptic and Koinoniac

Before space-time the only living beings (Father, Son, and Spirit) were living the Christian life. There is no human spirit, soul, or body. Just *spirit*! There is spirit and only spirit, and the realm is dimensionless. The Christian nurturing in this Christian "community" is confined totally to the fellowship of three persons in one. And these persons—in one person— are all in a spiritual realm. That spiritual realm is the only realm in existence.

The Christian life has been spirit, invisible, dimensionless— free of space and time—*from the beginning.*

Have you ever read a book that told you how to live the Christian life by ways that essentially by-pass space and time? Did anyone ever show you how to live the Christian life in the eternals? Did anyone ever tell you that you can fellowship with Jesus Christ *outside* of space and time?

That is where the Christian life began, and you and I have a right, by inheritance, to touch such an experience. The original home of the Christian life is in realms invisible, unseen and absent from a physical creation. That is, the "other realm" is the natural habitat of the Christian life. We can learn how to touch that realm. After all, that is where, and *how*, the Christian life had its origin, and that is where it still lives!

You are looking at the Father's will concerning how *pre-creation* Christians were to live the Christian life. Since we are having to invent terminology, let us refer to this as the *discovering* of the Christian life, the *learning* of the Christian life, the *laying hold* of the Christian life, and the *living out* of the Christian life. All this was located in a realm that had nothing to do with space and time. This is the Christian life founded on *revelation*—revelation flowing from the Father to the Son.

Apocalyptic

Does this flowing forth of revelation from the Father to the Son remain solely and exclusively the property of the Godhead? This is "revelating" between members of the Godhead—that is, the Father revealing Himself to the Son, the Son receiving revelation of His Father. Does this revelation then flow out from the Son to others?

The ingredients here are divine revelation and an exchange of divine fellowship.

Koinoniac

So far, all this wonder takes place in God—outside the confines of space, dimension, and time. The laying hold of the Christian life by means of an apocalyptic encounter. . .in realms unseen. The most primitive ingredients of Christian living: the Father revealing Himself to the Son, or, putting it another way, the Father and the Son fellowshipping.

What a way to increase the dimension of the Christian life!

First, revelation of Him and from Him, then fellowshipping with Him.

Of course, all of this is impossible for us! After all, the "Christian life" changed radically when God the Son became incarnate and entered space-time. Space-time alters the Christian life, after all! What was in the eternals is null and void down here! There can be no more of this particular kind of Christian relationship, Christian growth, and Christian living—by means of nothing but the fellowship of three spirit beings fellowshipping outside of time and space. This is eternity, territory of which earth has no claim.

So when the Lord Jesus came to earth, He had to start living the Christian life by "Plan B"?

Don't bet on it!

Still, that is surely not also for us! That kind of Christian life is not ours to know! Plan B must be for us.

There is a foreverness in God's way of doing things. *That* has been overlooked.

Traditional Ways to Live the Christian Life

Let's doubt.

For a moment let's doubt the accepted evangelical teaching we have been taught concerning the how of the Christian life.

After we list what we have been told, let's compare that approach with what took place in the Godhead, from the beginning.

First: Growth and victory come by cognitive, frontal-lobe study of the Scripture. You hardly even need a spirit to do this. That is, by the mental, intellectual acquisition of objective facts and information in Scripture—by *that* means you have the Christian life. Then, having learned what's there, go do it! This approach to Christian living is never advertised as intellectualism, but it ends up that way.

The element of other-realmness in our approach to Scripture simply does not exist. Perhaps we forgot that the author of the Christian life did not find His ultimate secret to living the Christian life by knowing the Scriptures.

Do know the Scriptures! But better, know the Author. Know Him, outside of realms seen. Know Him, in the invisibles.

Second: Acquisition of spiritual power.

You might know this by several other names: speaking in tongues, induement with power, the baptism of the Holy Spirit, etc. Pentecostalism, glossolalia, filled with the spirit, revival . . .these are all advertised as being able to give you instant power to live the Christian life! Whatever it is, it has "Made in the USA" stamped all over it. In the land of instant tea, instant milk, instant coffee, instant houses, instant heroes (not to mention instant heresy), it was inevitable that we come up with an instant Christian cure-all. The Christian life, trouble-free and crossless.

Third: Prayer. We cannot fault this. But when you actually step back and look at what we consider prayer to be, you see it is something virtually all one-sided. Surface. Shallow. The element of fellowship, the element of other-realmness, a relationship outside of space-time are not there. Let us dare ask this terrible question:

Does the way we pray have transformational qualities?

Witnessing. Tithing. Attending church. What else? All of the above elements—all stressful—for living the Christian life may offer some help; but in actual practice, all of these traditional methods usually turn out to have the nutritional value of a chunk of marble. Again, there is a present-day evangelical mind-set about these things which needs very close re-examining!

There are an awful lot of methods floating around out there. They have been advertised, and accepted, for centuries. But look around! After *centuries*, what is the result? Whatever your feeling about them, know this, they all pale in the presence of the relationship the eternal Son had with the Father!

Please, Lord, reconsider, for our sakes. This Plan B thing just isn't working down here! Could you make room for us—just a little—in that primordial way of how to live the Christian life? That original, primitive and very simple way found there in the Godhead, really looks appealing to us sitting down here in a three-dimensional world, surrounded by methods so old they have beards. What we have been chewing on all these years is neither nourishing nor satisfying. Could we join that fellowship, outside space-time? Just a little?

And if the outliving of the Christian life as practiced by God is so radically different from our evangelical ways, what must the Godhead's practice of *church* be!

Let's go now to Nazareth and see if there really is a Plan B.

5

In about the year 26 A.D. the population of Nazareth dropped. It lost *one* resident. Jesus left Nazareth.

During those first thirty years living in Nazareth, Jesus had been busy...doing what? He had been learning how to live the Christian life on earth! (He already knew how *to live the Christian life* in His Father, in the spirit realm.) But how to live it here on earth? Did His mother teach Him? Did He figure it out on His own? Did He learn it from the Old Testament? Or at the local synagogue?

Or is it just possible He *already* knew the secret to living the Christian life! To put it another way, did His Father reveal these things to Jesus as He grew—an indwelling Father re-teaching His now physically incarnate Son? Along the way, did the Father cause His Son to remember? The Father, inside Jesus, revealing the *how* to His Son from the inside?

Yes! Jesus' living out the Christian life on earth was a duplicate of His life in God in past eternity!

Let's go back to a barn in a village and watch this progression from the day Jesus was born until that time, at age 30, when He left home.

His Birth

The place is Bethlehem. The scene is a stable.

The eternal Son of God is about to take on the form of human flesh—God making entrance into the physical realm. On earth, He will be subject to space- time. His eyes will now see physical things rather than invisible things. Here on earth, everything is rock hard *visible*. Here He will grow. He will mature, passing from babe, to boy, to man. All this activity will take place in a realm filled with molecules. *Physical* reality. You know, the place where you live. The not-so-nice realm. The realm where living the Christian life doesn't work so well.

Did Jesus Christ have full spiritual consciousness at birth? Did He, lying there in that cradle, know that He was God incarnate? Was He just pretending to be a baby as far as consciousness was concerned?

No, of course not.

His human part had to go through a growth process. And that human part of Christ had to grow at the same pace it does for us. His soul life (His human life) passed through all the stages of growing up which *you* passed through.

Yes, but what of his divinity?

Some way, in the immutable mystery of God, it was decreed that Jesus' spirit, the seat of His divine nature, His divine life, would reveal itself within Him at the same pace as the growth of His human life.

Awareness and apprehension of what He was, as one divine, would come to Him in lockstep with the growth of His human life. Your Lord gradually became aware of who He was *spiritually* as He became conscious of His humanity.

(Let's hope that we are theologically accurate here, for we are in a place where few theologian's feet have ever bothered to tread.)

Your Lord was one hundred percent God and one hundred percent man. However, in Bethlehem He was a baby. As God, He would gradually discover what it was like to be man. As man, He would gradually discover that He was God. In both cases He was making awesome discoveries. In *both* cases He was discovering another life form inside Him. God discovering His humanity. Man discovering His divinity.

For the first time ever, there was a man here on earth who was getting used to the fact that the highest life form in existence was *in* Him, *and* one with Him. The human discovered Godness; the divine discovered humanness—two biological life forms growing up together in the presence of the knowledge of one another.

If that is not very clear, be at peace. We are never going to understand this matter fully. Your Lord was born with the divine nature and the divine life of His Father. . .inside Him.

Not so with us. You and I acquired the divine nature only at the moment of our salvation. Unfortunately, that mysterious and marvelous event took place in our lives long *after* we were well-versed in being human and in being fallen. But this fact does not lock us out of the Christian life as Jesus Christ knew it.

Our pathfinder Jesus the Christ, the God-man, discovered the Christian life as He grew up. From Bethlehem's cradle to Jordan's waters, He discovered the way to live the Christian life. But is that way different from the demand placed on us about how *we* are to live the Christian life? Or, are His and ours the same? His way, our way?

The Makeup of Jesus Christ

Biologically, just what is the content of Jesus the Christ? *First*, He had a part in Him which you and I did not have. More accurately, we were born with one part missing; He was not! *Second*, there was another part that was in Him and also in us; however, the part was functioning in Him, whereas in you and me, that part was inoperative.

One part was missing and one part was out of operation.

That part which was functioning in Him but inoperative in you before salvation is the human spirit. Your spirit had been more or less dead since Adam fell. The human spirit inside Jesus Christ was functioning perfectly, even at His birth.

What about the missing part? This "something" was not only missing in you and me, even Adam never had that element in him. That same *something* has been missing in all humans. Not so with this Bethlehem Child. The part was not missing. It was in Him.

What was that part? *Divine* life!

From His very inception, *the living God* indwelt this child named Jesus. That baby had the *indwelling* Father *inside* Him.

The point: Jesus Christ grew up with a sinless body and an undamaged soul. Those two elements made up the *human* side of Jesus Christ. Jesus also grew up with a living, functioning spirit. . .and God the Father *in* Him. That was the *divine* side of Him.

Divine life in Jesus Christ, *functioning*.

Here is the central question again: Does this give your Lord a Plan A in the business of how to live the Christian life, and us a Plan B?

Divine life was functioning in Him. He definitely had

Plan A for how to live the Christian life. Must we accept Plan B?

(Don't despair. We, a bit later—and, yes, even with a very fleshly body—received His life inside us. Eventually, we did become partakers of divine life!)

Growing up in Nazareth this incredible Jesus had a human spirit and a divine spirit made one. Such mysterious elements are not fully understood by us. This divine, invisible element does not belong to this realm. His spirit is not native to the physical realm but to another realm. He may be on earth, but He is drawing His resources for living the Christian life from "the other realm."

Let it be repeated: The outliving of the Christian life is not native to our realm. It is always lived out from the sources of the invisible, spiritual, non-dimensional realm. The natural habitat of the Christian life is the other realm. The Christian life is indigenous to—and matches—the spiritual realm.

The human spirit and the divine spirit are. . .well. . .*spirit*, and therefore belong to a realm where physical things are not. Grasp this in order to grasp spiritual realities: The invisible, spiritual realm is *not* bound by space and time, and it is the natural habitat of the Christian life.

The non-material realm has no measurable dimensions. You cannot measure nor find matter in the spiritual realm. It is dimensionless, being neither large nor small. Believe it or not, that fact profoundly affected Jesus' life on earth, and, once grasped, it profoundly affects your Christian life, too. We must look deeper into this overlooked yet crucial fact. In discovering other-realmness, we find God's way of doing things.

With that in mind, let's return to that carpenter shop.

40

6

When Jesus, age twenty-one, took His place in front of a bench in a wood shop, the living out of the Christian life moved out of the invisibles into space-time, into an earthbound man. From the time the Carpenter from Nazareth was twenty-one until He was thirty (18 A.D. to 27 A.D.), He lived not primarily by the acquisition of information. Not even religious information. Neither by His religious training, nor His human environment, nor its customs or social matrix.

His Christian experience came primarily by bursts of revelation. Revelation burst forth in a locatable place inside Him. That place was apprehended in ways wholly different from human intellect! This God-man touched spiritual reality by means of revelation and by fellowship. . .inside. Where is this geographically locatable place? (It is the same location whether the Son of God is in the heavens or on the earth.) It is in other realms, *and* inside a carpenter. It is in His spirit.

Other realms, invisible, non-dimensional, eternal, as well as the Carpenter's spirit, are as one. It was from this locatable place in Him that all things spiritual flowed forth. It was from there Jesus lived the Christian life. What a way to live the Christian life. Only God could have come up with this!

How different from all we have been exposed to about the *how*! But where does that put you?

Are you excluded? How are you supposed to live the Christian life? By memorizing Scripture, by going to a Christian school, by speaking in tongues, by. . .?

The day you were saved and received that *missing part* in you, that part has been located in other realms and at the same time in you.

We have seen the *how* of the Christian life in the Godhead, before creation. We have seen the *how* of the Christian life in the Son of God here on earth. We have seen Him adapt to being physical and to being captive in a space-time continuum. We see Him acquiring and adapting to a body and a soul.

When a creature who has been one hundred percent spirit and utterly divine comes to earth and acquires a body and soul. . .does He have to change His life style, His way of living the Christian life? Did God's ways of doings things change?

Jesus continued His contact with a non-physical realm and a spiritual continuum. He was on earth, yet He could remember the way of the Christian life before creation. Jesus remembered His former life style.

He will soon begin His ministry. Will a major change occur?

This *way* of Jesus as a young boy and a carpenter is precisely the same *way*, the same pattern, of eternity past in the Godhead. This is the pattern of the Godhead. It did not change one whit.

What is God doing, anyway?

He is introducing the Christian life to the planet Earth. You are seeing the Father's version of how a person is supposed to live the Christian life on this celestial ball.

Look carefully, though, and you will see the Father not only establishing the major tenets of the Christian life, but also training a church planter. Furthermore, you will see the most elemental aspects of church life becoming visible.

Yes, that simple fellowship going on in the Godhead in eternity past is the earliest indication of the ecclesia. That inner relationship of the Trinity is the first experience of church life ever to exist. That experience of church life is being brought to our planet. You are seeing the earliest foregleam of the church as you watch a Carpenter fellowshipping with His Father!

And while all this is going on, the Father is also raising up the first Christian worker! What a *philosophy of education*! What a carpenter's shop! It was a far, far better school than the one Mathias and Zephan were attending.

The *how* of God in raising up Jesus the worker will be replicated later by the Lord Jesus when He begins raising up twelve Christian workers.

Never forget, this church life is woven into the very nature and fabric of God. Living the Christian life and living church life are inseparable, part of one whole. And the way a Christian worker is supposed to be raised up was established by God in Nazareth.

In that earliest of all experiences of the church, a pattern emerges which He will never forsake. Nor can today's way improve upon it.

Watch.

7

Jesus had learned how to bring His experience of church life from the eternal realm into the earthly realm. He had proven that the Christian life worked, not only in the invisibles, but also in the physical world. It was, therefore, time for Him to begin His ministry.

At last He closed the door on His carpenter shop and bolted it.

But this is not all that beat in the breast of the young carpenter. He also learned *church life* in the eternals. He learned church life inside the Father, in fellowship with the Holy Spirit.

Jesus was trained, by the Father, to be a *Christian worker*. There were no other Christian workers on the earth. In fact, there were no other Christians living on the earth at that time. And there was no church life on the earth on that memorable day when He closed His shop.

He was about to change all that.

Before Jesus preached one word or healed one soul, He planned to gather around Himself men who would live in His presence. Here was the Son applying the Father's way of doing things—introducing that way to our planet so that men might live in His presence. Just as the Son lived in the Father's presence, so twelve would live with Jesus. It was God's way of doing things in Jesus' life! And Jesus' way of doing things in *man's* life!

We are looking at a man who (1) is Christian, (2) really knows how to live the Christian life, (3) has had a great deal of *previous* experience in church life, (4) has been called and trained in how to be a Christian worker, and (5) has a heart to train others to be Christian workers.

We are looking at one who actually experienced God's way of accomplishing *all* these things. Jesus is now passing on the *pattern.*

Just as the Father called Jesus, so Jesus in turn is about to call *twelve* men. The Father *sent* the Son when the training of the Son was complete in Him on earth. Later, the Son will call and the Son will *send* the twelve when *their* training is completed. That calling of a dozen men was noticed by no one. . .except the Father! . . .and the angels!

And what shall God and angels see?

God's way of doing things coming to earth!! Men living in Jesus' presence, as He had lived in the Father's presence.

Only a handful followed Him. Yet within that small band was the hope of *all* which God had envisioned *before* creation! Those twelve men encapsulated the reason for creation.

So far in this saga, have you seen much evidence of the way men today approach these same areas? There really isn't any similarity in God's way of doing things and the way we do those same things, is there?

Those men were fallen; there were no *eternals* to be seen

in them. Still, Jesus did not switch to Plan *B*.

These men, like you and like me, started out with no experience in *other realmness.* These twelve men were truly spiritual Neanderthals. Remember when they shoved parent and child out of the way when such people tried to come close to Jesus? This they did out of blind selfishness and arrogance, mixed with ignorance. They tried to stop everyone else from proclaiming the gospel except themselves! Like us, the twelve were very sectarian and denominational.

Furthermore, every one of these men was trying to impress Jesus. (He wasn't impressed.) They neither knew who He was, nor where He had been, nor what preparation He had passed through, *nor* His insight into fallen men and their fallen nature.

They needed four years in God's presence, plus (later) divine life within them and the Holy Spirit on them. This is not to mention a cross and the literal sight of a resurrected, ascended Lord. Even then they came through by a squeak.

We are all like these men. We need their kind of training.

At the beginning they had pledged undying devotion to Him, only to turn around, even after the resurrection, and go home. . .and go fishing.

It fell to Him to answer their foolish questions, get interrupted from sleep, and settle family squabbles. Some job for God, huh??

They watched His every move.

The blink of His eyelids was scrutinized by them. When the Pharisees walked into the room and verbally ripped Him to pieces, the eyes of the twelve never left Him. They watched His fingers, His face, His breathing. That is how closely He was scrutinized.

But God would have had it no other way.

He knew that they needed a basic, fundamental change. Actually, they needed a biological alteration. They needed to have their DNA biologically transformed. Anything less radical than that wouldn't work, not on men that damaged.

They needed inseminated divinity, a transformation that would begin at the center and continue all the way out to the circumference.

8

At the end of the first year of His ministry, Jesus began playing favorites. He made it clear there were twelve who were to be close to Him constantly. Outside this twelve, there were seventy. Beyond that a few hundred. Beyond that, nothing except the capricious.

Jesus actually ordered His entire life in such a way that all He did, all He said, all He was, all the circumstances He allowed into His life (and His reaction to those circumstances) existed to serve as training for those twelve men.

The smaller the crowd, the more effective the results. To these twelve men Jesus devoted most of three years of ministry. He staked the purpose of creation and the destiny of eternal history on them! He gambled all on the outcome of His spending three years in constant fellowship with just twelve men. Everything.

After the crowds went home, He talked to these men. For long hours He shared with them what He had done, why, and how. And from *where* He derived His source.

Frequently He slipped away from everyone except this small band, taking them to some remote place. Sometimes He talked, and sometimes He didn't. Sometimes He simply emitted His Father's presence. Those may have been the best moments of all for those twelve underachievers.

Pause: Is this the way *we* train workers?

Jesus' Value System

Of the thousands who heard Him during those three years, there were probably no more than five hundred who followed Him. For Him, that was as it should be.

Your Lord was not after numbers. He had come to establish a new "nation" on this planet. He envisioned a "nation" so well-established that it would outlast all other kingdoms. In fact, it would be so firmly founded, it would even outlast the planet! What good is it to have multitudes, yet have no one who, in time, could give to all these people that which His Father had given Him. He would pass all that on to twelve men.

What if there had not been those twelve men to pass on that marvelous pre-creation life, that marvelous pre-creation experience and also that very same experience relived in a carpenter's shop. All of that was gathered up and given to and experienced by some blue-collar workers in Galilee.

If you do not know the answer to the question, "what if there had been no such men to whom was passed on this fellowship with the Godhead," then just look around you today at a Christianity which knows no such men. The answer is everywhere. We are sorely missing just such men.

God give us back such men! God give us back the way Jesus Christ did things.

We have come to that place in our story where Jesus began

taking His past experience in the Godhead and passing it on to mortal men. The Father had begun a work in His Son. Now it was the Son's turn to begin a work in twelve men and to see that work going on here on our planet.

Jesus Christ concentrated His life and ministry on foundational things. Here are the foundation stones of the faith.

Please remember, this is not the modern day concept of *discipling*. How can one disciple others when he himself has not lived with one who has lived outside space-time? How can one disciple others who have never known experiential *ecclesia* life, first-century style? How can there be any real discipling by men when those men were never themselves raised up the way God raised up men. Discipling today can be reduced to a syllabus, a *how to* book, on how to disciple and how to be a disciple.

This isn't first-century style. Then what is it? It is *man's* way of doing things!

What Jesus did with twelve men was utterly unlike today's way of raising up Christians, or raising up the church, or raising up workers.

Jesus replicated His own experience in eternity, and He also replicated His experience in a carpenter shop. He placed those two experiences in twelve men. (To Jesus, *that* is discipleship.) And those two experiences of His are really *only one*. He did this so that those twelve men, who had touched the eternals, could one day do the same in the lives of three thousand people!

But His disciples were slow learners. (Are we not also?) Let's look further at teacher and disciple. Let's look at God's way of raising up men who are "hard of listening."

9

The twelve were "learning handicapped." (Nine or ten couldn't even read.) Can Jesus succeed in passing on to them all He had previously experienced? His task was to:

    (1) show twelve men how He *lived the Christian life* in the bosom of the Father,

    (2) show these men a church life experience which echoed a church life experience in Galilee that had been known *only* in the Godhead, and then

    (3) train these men to be Christian workers in ways remarkably similar to the ways His Father trained Him to be a Christian worker.

Yes! Jesus did it! He turned Galilee into a grand walking, moving classroom. He used all Galilee in preparing a little band of men to live the Christian life, to know church life and to become Christian workers. He gave them a living taste of original church life. (Heaven's version—not ours—of what *ecclesia life* really is.)

Twelve men, present *from the beginning*!

Beginnings are always crucial. The first beginning was Jesus with the Father in eternity. The second beginning was the man Jesus in a carpenter shop in Nazareth. Now this is another beginning—Jesus passing all these elements on to fallen men.

In stages one and two, Jesus Christ had been there from the beginning. In stage three, twelve men were there from the beginning. As we shall see, there will be more "from the beginning" stages.

We have seen the curriculum which the Father used so exquisitely in preparing His Son. Now watch the curriculum the Son uses to prepare His disciples!

The Son's way of doing things

Jesus' method cannot be duplicated by human means. No present-day book and no *biblical view of discipleship* is ever going to remotely touch what Jesus did in Galilee. The Father's method was for the Son to be with the Father. The Father's method was the Father!

The Jesus method was for the twelve to be with Him! It was that simple. Jesus' method was Jesus.

Years later, Paul's method of training eight Gentile workers would also be *Jesus*. *That* cannot be duplicated, at least not by human means. Not even if you combine *all* the present ways being used all over this planet! The present evangelical cannot imagine Jesus' way. And there is no *way* other than Jesus'. All else is less—less than straw.

The present-day concept of preparing a Christian worker has been used for well over sixteen hundred years, but it is *not* the concept of Jesus Christ. Today's ways surely look nothing like the way the Father raised up Jesus. One is head knowledge and is maddeningly impractical. The other is the expression of a life form: God's life form.

To repeat, Paul's way of raising churches or raising workers, or presenting the Christian life doesn't look remotely like our ways. Paul's way was a duplicate of Jesus' way. And Jesus' way was *God's* way of doing things!

Your Lord's method was simple: to gather twelve men around Him, let them live in the presence of Deity, and show those men *divine outliving*.

They watched Him relate to the Father daily. . .the way He had done in eternity past. And daily they got the general impression that something was going on internally in Jesus and that it was going to have to become something happening in them.

The twelve disciples spent most of their time no more than twenty feet away from the Lord. Jesus spent eternity plus thirty years being close to God. How close? Not twenty feet. Jesus Christ had spent His time and His eternity being *one* with the presence of God.

The twelve heard every word Jesus spoke, from His quiet talks to His outbursts against the Pharisees. They heard His conversation with a soldier. They heard His simple "thank you" for food being served. They even heard the breathing of His sleep. They saw His life style. They noted that His Father was the center of that life style, the center of His conversation and the center of His *all*.

Jesus never let anything turn into information or facts. Repeat: Nothing they got was ever facts. Nothing was information. It all had a touch of timelessness, of unseenness. Somehow, the twelve men figured out that the words He spoke were revelation, not teaching. Your Lord was a *revelator*, not a professor of facts. May you learn the difference. And may you be raised up by a man who is a revelator, not a word shuffler.

If revelation is so uniquely important, what is revelation?

To understand revelation, understand first what it is not! Revelation is not getting a word from God about when the world will end. Nor is it "God gave me a revelation that I should be driving a thirty-five foot limousine," or "I've just written a new epistle which belongs in the New Testament."

There is only *one* revelation. That is the revelation of *Christ*. For Christ, there is also only *one* revelation. As He told us, He came to *reveal* the Father.

When you fellowship with your Lord outside space-time, when you really touch Him, you may understand. And if you hear Him speaking, it will not be eschatological words, it will be Christological words. There is only Christological revelation.

If He reveals, He reveals *Himself.* Revelation *is* Christ. And you will come away from such a moment talking about your Lord, His wonder, His glory. That, and that alone, is revelation.

The classroom in Galilee got more intense, as we shall see. Watch the succession. And may God give back to us those things of which you are about to read.

10

    Now we move into deep waters. Because we have lost and forgotten God's way of raising up men in all these areas, we would be wise to take a close look at the three years of training which these men received.

    As you read, keep in mind that about twenty-five years later, a man named Paul raised up eight Gentile workers in this same manner. Paul showed those eight men:

      the Christian life, God's way

        church life, God's way

          the Christian worker, God's way

           training men, God's way

    A classroom called Galilee. The teacher, God incarnated. The means: Jesus taking twelve men through the same experience which He had passed through when being trained by the Father. Never again forget these ancient—and long-forgotten—ways. And may God give us back the Jesus way and the Paul way of raising men. . .of showing them the real *how* of living the Christian life. . .and *real church life*.

Here are some subjects the Lord taught which you may not find in today's curricula.

Suffering Persecution

A warning that ran like a flaming thread throughout all the Lord's words was that there would be the necessity of suffering and persecution.

Draw up a list of topics which are *not* emphasized in today's training of a worker! On that list you will find *being persecuted.*

Nothing comes through as a greater shock to a young man starting out to serve the Lord than the fact that people say and do vicious things. Young workers are always shocked. Yet, even that encounter should never be known as persecution.

Most men are never truly persecuted for their ministry. Criticized, yes. Gossiped about, yes. But when it comes to physical endangerment and actual life-threatening situations, that kind of persecution is usually reserved for Christians outside the organized church.

And the cross?

The cross is, was, and forever will be, a rarely-mentioned subject. How is it that we all seem to get the universal impression that bad things are not supposed to happen to us Christians?

There are two events which will fill a man's life, from the first day he begins to minister Christ (or minister His church), which will continue on forward until the day the worker dies. One of these events is persecution. The other will either be division or the constant specter thereof.

Those two events are also the two elements most likely to eventually destroy Christian workers. (Not to mention the rest of us!)

May God's called men have the privilege of seeing a Christian worker being crucified! We desperately need to see such things. Why? Because, if you become a Christian worker you *will* be crucified. And, if you are to be crucified, you need to have a previous example. You need to know the "how to" of being crucified.

May young men then have the privilege of being present to see *you* being crucified. And may you show them how to be crucified in a way that exalts *the divine way of being crucified.*

Be assured that most Christian workers refuse to be crucified. Instead, they declare war on their would-be crucifiers. The few who allow crucifixion to happen to them rarely demonstrate the grace we need to see when we watch a man being crucified.

Be crucified in the Jesus style.

Jesus was aware of man's tendency to persecute and of our valiant effort to hold on to the idea that bad things are not supposed to happen to God's people.

Jesus made it very clear to the disciples: "Your ministry will be refused." He was also aware that His servants would always be shocked when persecuted, and that they would always be unprepared in knowing how to survive persecution.

The Lord Jesus made it clear that they could expect to be hated, lied about, scourged, and hauled in before every kind of government, there to be charged with every kind of crime. The Lord Jesus also made it clear that He expected them, in the midst of such trials, to take the opportunity to testify of Him. The twelve got a good foundation in what to expect. After all, they saw how much trouble Jesus got Himself into. He turned to them in one of those moments and said to them,

"A servant is not above His master, is he?"

They had a moment to reflect. These twelve servants had heard their master being called the son of a devil, illegitimate, a blasphemer, a drunk, and demon possessed. Gradually, they began to realize that they were also going to be called all these things, too. He was hated; they would be hated—in the same manner, with the same intensity.

Jesus provided them with a ringside seat into what it was really like to be a Christian worker.

There was another quality which Jesus exemplified. It had to do with losing!

Learning to Lose

Virtually any Christian leader will do everything in his power to keep the wavering from leaving. What are such men doing? They are trying to keep their group from getting smaller. Anything to keep the numbers. If a brother in the group is desiring to go somewhere else, the leaders will almost certainly warn, ridicule, or demean.

Men trying to keep their followers is the source of a large number of present Christian disasters. Trying to keep people from leaving is the mother of all scare tactics. In fact, trying to keep converts, trying to keep the numbers, is one of the worst sources of bad conduct found in Christian workers. Men trying not to lose their attendees can get *very* ugly. Such conduct simply indicates the cross has never been in their hearts. They have never been taught to lose. They have not learned to lose.

This was not the way of Jesus Christ. Over the last two thousand years, He stands almost alone in the list of Christian workers who never tried to keep a crowd. *Failing* and *losing* are two of the most overlooked *pillars* of the Christian faith.

Instead of trying to win, or to keep, He showed those twelve men how to *lose*. If His inner circle kept getting smaller, He did not seem to notice.

How could He do such a thing? After all, He was in a very small time frame—three years! It was because He knew who He was, that He could do this. May God give the church more men so uniquely trained that they know who they are! Jesus Christ knew what He was doing. He had the assurance of His *preparation*. Of His unique *training*. Of His *call*. And of His *sending*. May His tribe increase. (His tribe *will* increase if we should happen to return to God's way of doing things.)

Men who run after their converts, or who *scare* them in order to *keep* them, are insecure. Very insecure. They are men not familiar with God's way of doing things. Jesus Christ was not insecure. He could lose.

God give us men who know they have settled these four things, firmly settled them in their lives to the point they are at peace: Call, training, sending, and a willingness to embrace loss. And all this in the context of the raising up of the church.

It is our lot, sirs. . .to lose. . .and lose. . .and lose again.

Sometimes it even seemed that He pressed this point unnecessarily. He seemed to press to the limit with men. There once came a very fragile moment when He could have lost every one of His twelve. Instead of letting that tense moment pass, He chose that time to press His point as far as it could be pressed. He invited them to leave!

He lived in the shadow of loss. Your Lord lived by "He who keeps, loses; he who loses, gains." And twelve men noticed.

This example, this life style—this divine life style—is something today's way of training cannot provide.

The point is this. Those twelve men heard Him speak, then watched Him live what He spoke! Or, put another way, they watched someone live by a life not human. They watched a man live by divine life. By an upside-down value system. It wasn't easy to grasp, but His upside-down look at things and His upside-down way of living profoundly affected them. God, give us men like this again.

We have a need: young men who watch a Christian worker live by divine life. Men who watch a man live by an upside-down value system. We need men who have seen men suffer the loss of everything. We need men who have seen men willingly mount the cross.

Remember, though, that this was not His stopping point. They also saw Him fellowshipping daily with His Father. They saw Him doing on earth what He had done in the eternals.

Experiencing Church Life

Jesus did two incredible things which get overlooked; yet those two things were the heart, center, and core of His work on earth. They may be overlooked, but that does not make them less important.

Jesus Christ introduced those twelve men to real church life. He showed them (1) how to experience church life and (2) how to raise up church life.

Dear Lord, give us such men again—men who have *been in* that pattern. God give us men who have known the life of the body of Christ before beginning to give church life to others.

Watch the pattern:

    church life in the Godhead

    church life in a Carpenter's shop

    church life with Christ and twelve men

    church life with twelve men and 3000 new converts

Ecclesia life is not native to our planet. The fellowship of divine life between those who have divine life and live by divine life was, and is, natural only to the eternal. But the pattern, the experience, the "how to" of ecclesia life did get into our world: church life first in Nazareth, and then tasted in Galilee and Judea by twelve fallen men living with God.

Herein is the great stumbling block of our age, maybe of all ages. Perhaps, more than anything else, it is the unwillingness of men—men called of God—to stop what they are doing and sit down and learn. . .learn church life! Men living today, men called of God, seem almost unanimously unwilling to sit down and experience church life before ministry. Certainly they should have the experience before they run out to raise up a church!

Men called of God are ready and willing to start something called a *house church* but utterly unwilling to first be a learner in church life. The house church invariably collapses or ends up in the world of sacerdotalism.

Not so Christ; He learned. Not so, the twelve; they were willing! They learned. And we are about to see other men who came after the twelve who were also willing—willing to learn Christ, willing to experience church life, and willing to sit at the feet of men who had previously learned! Their names were Barnabas, Philip, Stephen, Agabus, Justus, Silas. Later, Paul. And then the Gentile workers: Titus, Gaius, Secundus, Tychicus, Trophimus, Sopater—all first-century workers—all knew church life before being sent! And, afterward, most became church planters. Where are called men who are willing to sit, willing to learn Christ, willing to be in church life, and willing to learn from the ones who came before them?

By the way, if you wish to know how hard it is to learn church life, just watch those twelve erstwhile men struggle with their embryonic experience of the ecclesia.

But for now, return to Galilee. There in that province the fellowship of the Godhead opened its doors and let fallen but redeemed men join in the fellowship of the Godhead.

The Unchanged, Unchangeable Pattern

The pattern had not changed. Jesus was showing these men how He had lived the Christian life. . .in the Godhead, back before creation.

Dare we hope to find men who can teach us how to have such a relationship with Jesus Christ? Do such men exist? Look for men who grew up in Christ. . .in the body of Christ . . .and I don't mean in the traditional church setting, *or* in any untraditional but legalistic setting.

It is remarkable that when the Lord finished with the twelve, they could do, and did, with three thousand new converts what they had seen their Lord do in their own lives.

Thank God, those twelve men eventually learned the way to live the Christian life. . .the only way. *The way*. And it wasn't Bible study that got them there! It was an internal thing, an eternal and invisible thing, a thing that belonged to other realms. It was because they lived in God's presence.

Those were twelve very blessed men, were they not? They were being allowed to see how to live the Christian life by watching One who related to an indwelling Father. And they were seeing how the greatest Christian worker of all worked! And they were being trained by the perfect Christian worker. And the training they received from Jesus had upon it the flavor of the training Jesus received from the Father.

Teachers in Bible schools and seminaries, standing behind desks, do not and cannot do this. Certainly we cannot pass on to others what we have never previously done, what we have not seen or heard, nor heard of, nor even thought about!

It was important that a small band of men be left on this earth who knew how to live the Christian life the way the Godhead lived it. We could do with another such band of men.

It was important that a small band of men be left on this earth who knew how to prepare future workers the way the Father had prepared the Son and the way they themselves had been trained. We could do with another such band of men.

It was important that a small band of men be left on earth who had seen and experienced true ecclesia life. They had, these twelve men with Jesus their center. We could do. . .

Remember, you never know ecclesia life except as it leads you to a bloody, destructive and annihilating cross!

That is exactly where knowing Christ and knowing ecclesia life led these twelve men!!

It was only after that cross and after resurrection—His *and* theirs—that the birth of the church on this earth could happen.

11

For forty glorious days after the resurrection Jesus lived among the twelve. The twelve lived with a *resurrected* Lord. You might call that their graduation present!!

Confident that He had done His work well, He then *departed*. No longer was He with them visibly.

Would the apostles be able to raise up a church that was virtually a repeat of their three-year corporate experience with Christ, without ritual, with Christ always at the center? Could they pass that *pattern* on to others just as He had passed it on to them? It was passed on to them by the Godhead.

Could they reproduce the Galilean experience they had—the experience of Christ living in the midst of men? Could they pass on this wonderful embryonic church life experience to a new generation of people who had never seen Jesus Christ, nor heard Him personally? Could they pass on to such people the experience of Christ, invisible, living in their midst?

Could they pass on to others *their* version

of living the Christian Life? Could those twelve ever hope to train a new generation of workers? Some of those questions would soon be answered in Jerusalem. Look for the answer in a place called Solomon's Porch, and in living rooms throughout Jerusalem. Later, look for that answer as the church came into being in villages and towns scattered throughout Judea.

Yes, the ecclesia *would* be born. And Jesus Christ *was* present in men. He was *present* in those gatherings. But what of a new generation to continue the work? Would there be church planters after the twelve?

Could there be a third generation of *workers*? Would the pattern hold? Could a third generation of men:

    (1) learn how to live the Christian life

    (2) know and experience church life

    (3) be called, trained and sent to be church planters

    (4) wonder of wonders, dare we hope that they and even future generations might someday do it *all* yet *again*!

All this would be after the pattern. All, God's way.

This third generation of workers able to raise up a fourth generation of Christian workers without forsaking the pattern—that's the most mind-boggling thought of all!

Between the resurrection and the Day of Pentecost, there are no more than fifty days. Listen to what Jesus declared during that time concerning the continuation of the pattern, concerning God's way of doing things:

"The Father sent me; now *in that same way* I send you."

What did the Lord mean? We now have an idea of what "in the same way" means. But what is meant by "called," and what is meant by "sent"?

Called—Trained—Sent

Somewhere in eternity, Jesus had been called by the *Father*—called to that with which we are all so familiar. (Or are we?) He was called to His task before the fall. *Before* the beginning! He was to make us *one*.

Then, beginning in the womb of a woman and growing up in Nazareth, He was *prepared* by the *Father*. Finally, there on the shores of the Jordan River, when a voice from out of a door in the heavenlies spoke, Jesus Christ was *sent*. . .by the *Father*.

Twelve men had been with Him at that beginning. It was in about 26 A.D. that these twelve men were *called* by the Son. Then, for three years they were *prepared* by the Son in much the same way as the Father had prepared the Son. Then, in about 30 A.D., just before the festival of Pentecost in Jerusalem, the twelve were *sent* by the Son.

What the Father had done in sending Jesus Christ, now Jesus Christ did in sending twelve men. The pattern was passed on. God's way of doing things was unchanged from the first motion on.

Again, you see the oneness, the integration, the identification. The pattern. You see the divine life style stretching from the eternals into the first-century saga and on to the close of that saga. It continued unbroken.

Lord, restore that pattern!

After these twelve men were sent, the Holy Spirit accompanied them wherever they went. Christ would indwell them as the Father had indwelt Jesus. . .wherever they went.

We have now seen two beginnings: Christ, called before the beginning of creation; the twelve, chosen in Christ before the foundation of the world and called at the beginning of Jesus' ministry.

Two things about His training of the twelve which are principles of His that went on to be established throughout the first-century, but which are almost never noticed:

(1) It is important that men called of God have the experience of being there at the beginning; and

(2) The Christian life and all its facets are always found in a corporate setting. The Christian life is an ecclesia matter.

It is now time to see the birth of the church in the first century.

12

It is Sunday; the time is 5 a.m. The day is a holiday called the celebration of Pentecost. It is also the day the *sending* becomes reality.

Twelve men, in Jerusalem, facing a mammoth task. But they are prepared! The root of their training predates creation and includes having lived with the earth's only Christian!

Before we go on, let's pause and look at the stages that have brought us to this point.

Stage 1: The Godhead in eternity.

Stage 2: God in Christ.

Stage 3: God and twelve fallen, redeemed men in Galilee of Judea.

Stage 4: Twelve recipients of Stages 1, 2, and 3. . .plus 3,000 new believers.

For over three years they had lived with the only inhabitant of earth who knew what church life, Godhead-style, looked like. They knew *the* one man who had experienced church life! This man was also the earth's *only* Christian worker, and the twelve had lived with

Him. They had missed nothing. They had been with Him in Galilee. . .*from the beginning*!

Their instructions? Duplicate these three years' experiences as nearly as possible in other Christians. Replicate the entire *Christian sphere* as they had learned it from Jesus Christ. Take the Christian life and *genuine* church life, and move it to stage four. Later, raise up workers. Do all this in a way not too dissimilar to the way the Father did, and the way Christ did. The pattern. The life style. The way of the Godhead. Follow the path. "Carry out your work according to how you experienced it in Galilee." As to ministry? (Somewhat unique, especially if compared to ministry of the last 1700 years.) Present Christ. Always present Christ.

Jesus had ministered *Himself.* The twelve came up with a sensational idea: They would minister Jesus Christ!

Twelve ordinary men had observed, at close range, that Jesus Christ was involved in an interchange with the eternals. That is a very unusual plane upon which to live the Christian life. They knew this was His secret! These men knew *the* secret!

Twelve men had watched the greatest worker of all time work. They experienced church life *with* that worker.

Now, observe the pattern as it continues. This time it is not Jesus who is the Christian worker. It is ordinary men. Men not too dissimilar to you and me. (Less educated than we are, of course. I leave it to you to decide who has the edge in the presence of that fact.)

Jesus began His ministry for the purpose of increasing the number of men and women with divine life in them. In the beginning there had been only *three*! He came here prepared to increase the number who fellowshipped with the Godhead.

When He started the number of fallen men who were living by and experiencing divine life was zero.

Jesus came to earth to bring *ecclesia life*—the Godhead version, which had its origins in the eternals—to earth. He came to bring the *community* of the Godhead to earth. He began His work here on earth *for the church*.

The *worker* began His work. The church planter stepped out of another realm and came here and dared plant the embryo of that ecclesia. . .here. . .on this dusty ball!

Then He *left*! He got up and. . .left!

Observe the forward flow of *that* pattern.

The twelve men enter an upper room. They have a history, have a perspective, have a spiritual relationship to the eternals which is not too unlike that which the Son of God had with His Father! Surely, nobody who has ever walked on this earth has ever had such an experience or such equipment to work with as these men had!

They had seen Him glorify His Father. Eventually they reached a point of overflow where they could not help but glorify the Son. Twelve master builders, experienced in church life, trained by the greatest builder of all. On the day of Pentecost these twelve unusually trained men went to work.

(All Christian workers should follow *this* pattern, and this pattern only!)

Do you remember how the Holy Spirit was placed on Jesus at the beginning of His ministry? Now the twelve are going to have the Holy Spirit placed on them.

First Christ *in* them on the day of resurrection. Now the Holy Spirit *on* them at 9 a.m. on the day of Pentecost. The Holy Spirit will now replicate *His* work! *First in* them, and then—after preparation and brokenness—*on* them.

After they are clothed *upon* with the Holy Spirit, are they going to:

    (1) start a para-church organization?

    (2) begin pell-mell blitz evangelization?

    (3) scatter out all over the planet?

    (4) become pastors?

No! They are going to do what had been done according to the pattern.

They knew, experienced and lived in *church life* before they ever dared to plant a church. Then they *planted.*

They also knew how to live the Christian life the Jesus way, and they lived it. . .the Jesus way. Then they exhibited it . . .just as their Lord had done before them.

Not exactly a modern-day version of "how." This is God's version of "how." (For some odd reason it is extremely hard to get men today to look away from the modern version and follow God's way of doing these things.)

The twelve were going to plant the ecclesia on earth. Like their Lord, their first order of business was to become *church planters*! They, like their Lord, were being *sent*. First called, then trained, *then* sent.

Jesus was *sent* to this planet to plant the embryo church here. The Son then called and trained twelve men. Now the Son has *sent* the twelve to carry out this same unmovable, eternal purpose:

    (1) to invite men to fellowship with the Godhead

    (2) to give church life to men. . .on earth. . .as it was known and experienced in eternity by the Trinity.

Jesus Christ knew how to live the Christian life before He shared anything with anyone. Jesus Christ knew the experience of church life *before* He gave the church to anyone on this planet. Jesus Christ was fully *trained*, by sitting at the Father's feet, *before* He became a Christian worker. Jesus Christ did not raise up workers until He had experienced the full scope of being trained as a Christian worker. . .and then working as a Christian worker.

And the twelve, did they follow that pattern?

The twelve learned the Christian life before sharing it, knew church life before raising up the church, and were trained by a church planter before they became Christian workers. And they will prepare other men only after years of experience in being church planters.

Sir, follow the pattern.

How far were they sent? To New Zealand? (New Zealand is the farthest point from Jerusalem on this planet.) No! They were sent. . .*downstairs*! And for the next six years, twelve men will go nowhere. Just downstairs! Just Jerusalem. Six years!

(Never tell that to a non-demoninational para-church organization. They send young people out to the ends of the earth—after just thirty days! And they do so because they tell their recruits that *this* is the way the twelve did it! No sir! This is the way *men* do it.)

It appears that God is not all that driven to convert the world. He would make a poor para-church worker, and an even worse modern-day missionary or evangelist.

In the coming weeks, three thousand people will watch men who have divine life in them. Six thousand eyes will watch those men draw upon *life within*. The three thousand will see a *way* that is amazingly similar to the way Jesus did things.

It turns out that these twelve men are very good at fellowshipping with the Lord Jesus, be it with Him in Galilee, or be it *with* Him. . .*inside* their rib cage.

13

On *Sunday* there were three thousand new people who had divine life in them.

But now it is *Monday*. The twelve have instructed the three thousand "new life carriers" to meet them at Solomon's Porch.

What do the twelve do after the three thousand have arrived there? Guess!

They lift up Jesus Christ!

When the new believers listen. . .they are soon awash in the glory which is Jesus! What they hear fills their spirits. The twelve show three thousand people *Jesus Christ*. They show three thousand souls how to fellowship with this Lord, how to experience this indwelling Christ both personally and corporately. They also show them how to fellowship with the twelve, and how to fellowship with one another.

Sound familiar?

No, dear reader, this just does not happen in this age, among us evangelicals. (In fact, such ministry has not prevailed throughout the entire Protestant era.)

Oh, by the way, such encounters so overwhelmed these three thousand that living in Christ spontaneously produced church life. Church life is not an organizational thing; it is an organic thing. Its experience is found in what people do, spontaneously, after they have an encounter with Christ. The next six years, the three thousand sat there in Jerusalem without moving. Further, the twelve *never* asked anyone to be soul winners or to evangelize.

They had learned from Jesus, who, in three years, sent out the twelve on just one *practice run*. Two weeks the twelve "worked" throughout all their three years. So, the twelve asked for no "work" from the three thousand. . .*not* during *all* those six years.

These twelve men really did follow in His steps. They did not rush *new converts* into *soul-winning* (or any other kind of Christian service. Leaders of para-church organizations take note.)

The pattern is holding. God's way of doing things is alive, in Jerusalem. This "way" has flowed into the hands of mere men. Church planters who are of the fallen race of Adam have begun to glorify the Son here on earth *in the Godhead style*.

May it begin again. And then forever be!!

For the next six years, the apostles could have turned those three thousand believers into soul winners, drained them dry, burned them out. . .the way our para-church organizations do to enthusiastic young people!

Evangelize the world? Contrary to all you have been taught, our concept of evangelism did not happen then, in any way, shape or form—not by the twelve, not in Jerusalem. And when evangelism finally came:

(1) it happened a lot more gradually than you have been told; and

(2) the end purpose of all first-century evangelism was to bring forth the *church*. (Not "churches" as we know them.) Evangelism, first-century style, brought forth an organic community of believers. Ecclesia!

What did happen in Jerusalem? The twelve gave those three thousand people. . .Jesus! For *six* years!!

Reread the record. *All* evangelism in Jerusalem was done by the twelve. By the twelve alone, and no one else! If there was any physical or emotional draining, it was the twelve who were drained. Put *that* in your teachings about evangelism.

Now where do you suppose they got that concept of: (1) centering on Jesus Christ, *and* (2) not working the stuffing out of new believers.

Working yourself to death in the Lord's work is the exclusive territory of *church planters*. Twelve men laid hold of this concept in Galilee while watching a *true* worker work. In Galilee, your Lord had done it all.

And where did Jesus get the idea of "slow" when it came to *training* workers? And to *sending* workers out? And where did your Lord get the just-watch-do-nothing concept? He got *this revolutionary* idea from the Father. Jesus Christ beheld the Father for an eternity plus thirty years *before* He ministered. This is the *only* true pattern there is. And that pattern flowed unbroken and unchanged throughout all the first Christian century.

New converts take note. You are supposed to be growing in Jesus Christ. . .nothing else! In the depths of Jesus Christ . . .in oneness with Him. But most of all, whatever you receive is supposed to come to you within the community of *church life*. Nowhere else.

The twelve had sat on a rock in Galilee, a floor in Judea, a synagogue stool in Capernaum. Twelve men had *watched* while Jesus Christ *took the entire burden of the work*. He did the work. He received the abuse. Virtually all the Christian work performed during the three years those men received their training was done by *Jesus*. . .while the twelve men *beheld*! While twelve men listened!! That is virtually the only thing they did. The little which they did do while Jesus was with them was nothing but a "dry run." Two weeks, total. Nothing else!!

Jesus Christ did all the preaching, witnessing, soul winning, healing, counselling, and teaching. He made *all* the decisions. They sat and listened, learned and absorbed. At the end of three years, they were awash with the *practical*. *(They were also awash with the spirit.)* The philosophy of "how to be trained" was nil. It was the most practical training ever received by man.

By the way, this type of learning is called "ped-learning" in the Greek—learning by walking. Peripatetic learning is nonexistent in Christianity today, yet it was the Jesus style. (Peripateticism refers to students walking alongside an itinerant teacher as he moves about from place to place.)

Now, it is *Jerusalem time*. The twelve do likewise. For six years (which is about three more years than Jesus' time of living with the twelve), these men dispensed the *indwelling* Jesus Christ.

This time it is the *twelve*, not the three thousand, who do all the preaching, teaching, counseling, and soul winning. . . while six thousand eyes and ears listen, learn, behold, absorb and experience. They will soon be awash in both the practical and spiritual.

Always remember: The three thousand *experienced*. They *experienced* Christ! *Experienced* church life. They were not pushed into burnout.

The reason the three thousand experienced Christ was because twelve men knew how to teach men how to experience Christ. The twelve had experienced an indwelling Lord; now three thousand did.

Watch that pattern flow!

All the vicious criticism and persecution? It fell on the twelve. Not on *anyone* else. The twelve were a shield to the ecclesia. That's the way it is supposed to be in the lives of church planters. That was fine with them. They *expected* no less. They had been well-trained. They knew how to handle persecution, criticism and innuendo. How did they know?

They had watched how God handled Himself when God was being persecuted.

Let's see how things went for the 3,000 during the next six years. See if you detect a pattern.

14

We have seen how three thousand—with their mouths wide open and their eyes bulging—watched how twelve men so effortlessly handled abuse, criticism, hate, trial and prison. And how the twelve lived the Christian life. *And* how they raised up the ecclesia. *And* how the twelve did *not* call on the 3,000 to serve the Lord.

In all the next six years, the only thing any of those thousands of new converts did was to take over the serving of food. Until that time, the twelve had *even done that.*

Dear young Christian, go join a Christian organization today; see if you receive your training in this way. Join any organization, any church, any Bible school, any seminary. First-century style simply cannot happen there. There are thousands of reasons you cannot get Jesus' pattern of training. One reason is: it's not Christ-centered or in the church under a church planter.

We are unfamiliar with the way divine life does things. We are unfamiliar with the life style of the Godhead. Here is God's way, lost for 1700 years.

May our evangelical mind-set crumble!

To you who run the religious organizations of our day, here is a question. (Please do not answer this question with a Bible verse because there is a Bible verse for everything.) Why is it that you work young Christians into a life-ruining case of burnout? In so doing, you deny the young people whom you push so hard the one most valuable experience. . .church life. You also leave them with *nothing* of the *depths* of the Christian life.

These young Christians see you living the *external*. You are bent on evangelization. Period. Grit, groan, push, work, sweat, preach, read Bible, pray. . .where is the Godhead in this burnout formula?

That is not how Jesus Christ demonstrated the way to live the Christian life. Nor did He in any way use *your* way of training men. Nor did the twelve. Both Christ and the twelve gave God's people a Christian walk that was *other dimensional*. They gave God's people real, honest-to-goodness church life, trained church planters, and trained them slowly, inside church life.*

*Timothy is often used as a counterexample. But watch the chronology. If Timothy got saved at twenty, he was about thirty when he began his Christian service. (And Timothy's work was church planting.) That gave Timothy ten years of beholding, ten years at the feet of a church planter. Timothy was trained the old-fashioned way. . .the peripatetic way. Teacher and learner did not use a rostrum and chair. They walked. The church planter demonstrated; his learner walked and watched. The teacher lived his work; his disciple followed along, watching. Put that at the top of the list of things needing to be restored.

It is proper that the older worker do the debilitating work. He is, after all, a worker. It is proper that the younger one watches!

May our evangelical mind-set never recover!

This is an ancient Christian tradition. If traced back to its origin, this way of learning would lead you all the way back to the Godhead, before creation!

This is the way the Godhead does things!

There is no New Testament precedent for using youth to evangelize. The time God gives for being young is for learning Christ. Youth is for living in church life, and only in church life, and watching. Watching *church planters*.

Dear Christian leaders of organizations which are full of young people in their early twenties, how will you explain all of the unscriptural things you have young people doing?

Evangelizing the world is the exclusive territory of church planters and churches, with converts placed in real, organic, indigenous (non-American-style) church life.

Do you know where the vast majority of those precious young people will be ten years from now? They will be burned out. And scattered. Unaccounted for. You *know* that. Then why do you persist in a methodology that never existed in the first century and has most of its roots and mind-set coming from the 1880's when "evangelize the world" began to be promoted.

As you know, this non-church concept of evangelism—this blitz evangelism set solely on saving men from hell—has no first-century equivalent.

Young people, if you work for the Lord in your *youth* the way those twelve grown men did in Jerusalem, it will *destroy* you—spiritually, physically, emotionally, morally, psychologically. . .and perhaps permanently.

All those verses they taught you about evangelism and how you *had* to evangelize. . .every verse you heard quoted in *all* the four gospels. . .were only spoken to the twelve. . .*not* to you!

The great commission. . .that is an even worse corruption of Bible exegesis. It was spoken to twelve church planters. Here is the even more neglected fact: That quote by Jesus was a prophesy, a *prediction*, rather than a command: "You (twelve) *will* go. . .to the ends of the earth."

If we trust the early records of Christian history (Eusebius of Caesarea—circa 300 A.D.), all the twelve church planters were old by the time they finally got out "into all the world." Even then they left Israel mostly because the Roman legions pushed them out.

Note this. In those six years in Jerusalem, though the demands which came upon those twelve men had escalated virtually out of the bounds of human endurance, still God's people only *watched!*

Young Christians ought not to serve the Lord; young people should *experience* Christ in the church. They should fellowship with God the Father and with His Son, Jesus Christ. In the ecclesia, in a true expression of church life! And their role models should be *church planters!*

That alone, nothing else. No place else. No one else.

Let's look at just how important it was—in Century One—for those first *church* members to learn and *not* serve. To learn Christ, to know and experience church life. . .both so necessary for all Christians. . .and especially for future workers.

Will there be yet another motion, a stage *five* in this incredible drama? Does God's way of doing things reach beyond Christ and even out there *beyond* the twelve and the three thousand?

15

The results of this very unusual approach to Christianity? Read the results for yourself. Out of those three thousand would come the next generation of Christian workers. . .Silas, Stephen, Philip, Barnabas, Justus, Agabus.

As we move on, remember the twelve were all present at *the beginning* of the Lord's ministry. The three thousand were all present *at the beginning* of the birth of the church.

Next, those men just listed got to see a church born—*at the beginning*. They had the privilege of being in a church birth! If you are called of God, may you be so blessed as to be an ordinary brother at the birth of a church. And may it be real ecclesia life that you experience. And may a church planter be around when it all begins. (And, to be doubly blessed. . .may the church planter have grown up in church life, himself.)

Those six men just named watched church planters plant. They were witnesses to the "how" of church planting! Six men, present at the ground-breaking ceremony.

Four years earlier, the twelve had started

out with Jesus at the very time Jesus had begun His ministry. They saw the embryonic church. They were present at the birth of the first experience of church life this planet had ever seen.

Dear reader, label these "methods" as very good. The results were very good too. May this be our pattern!! It is the way the Godhead does things.

Now let's look at how old these twelve men are. Especially in the light of the present-day consumption of young people by para-church organizations. In seeing this part of the story we discover the importance of being over thirty years of age.

The twelve began following Jesus in their early or middle-thirties. They were the *second generation* workers. (Jesus was the first.) There is now a third generation of workers, but they did not begin to appear until after the twelve were about forty years of age.

At age forty-plus, the twelve men who were sent to evangelize the world finally got up and departed Jerusalem. They finally got a chance to fulfill the "uttermost" part of their sending.

How far did they go?

To the nearby Judean countryside! No more than thirty or forty miles.

Age forty is a pretty good bench mark year for all Christian workers. You might also begin, as did the twelve, in *your own* country rather than Saudi Arabia or Afghanistan! And remember, know church life *first*.

Please include all the above in your teaching on evangelizing the world. Put this in your para-church instructor's manual. (No doubt your organization would collapse. After all, the cornerstone of your organization is using youth for evangelism.)

Do you want to be an evangelist? Put all these ingredients in your life *before* you become an evangelist!

First-century evangelists *all* knew church life before becoming evangelists. They were functioning as simple local brothers *before* they took on any inter-church function. This is why they were able to survive those six stress-filled years before going into Judea. There were more than three thousand people making constant demands on them. (Eventually, *twenty* thousand or more.) There was lying, cheating, criticism all around, gripes, complaints inside and persecution outside. That is all hard to survive. How did they know how to respond?

For three years they had been watching a first-class Christian worker go through all those stresses. They had even learned how to be crucified in the way that divine life goes through crucifixion!

Would you prefer being trained by men like that? You would? Then what are you doing in seminary? (Or is it a para-church organization you belong to? Or whatever!)

Twelve men knew all about living by means of a biological life form that was higher than human life—and they experienced that within the ecclesia. That is the "how" which God intends for all of us.

That is where men called of God belong. These are the experiences every worker needs to have the honor of *watching* happen during his apprenticeship. Do you know any Christian worker or church planter who knows how to be crucified?

The twelve knew one who did!

You have a right to learn from such men! If God has called you, accept no substitute. This is the only proper way of being trained. And if you are a Christian desperate for church life. . .then have church life by these means only. Accept no substitutes.

May you see the Christian life. . .the Godhead way. May you be in ecclesia life *from the beginning*. And may that ecclesia be raised up the way Jesus raised up the church, the way the twelve raised up the church, the way Paul raised up the church.

The way God does things.

And if you are a young ministerial student called of God, may you be delivered from the way men train young ministers in our age. May you be raised up by a church planter whose style is not unlike that of the Father, of Jesus, of all the first-century planters!!

Church planters are the ones, the only ones, who are supposed to raise up new workers.

The next stage, stage five, now begins to emerge. As they come into view, will we continue to see the pattern? Will we see things still being done the way the Father and Son did things?

16

Persecution hit Jerusalem. Suddenly, everything changed. The Jerusalem believers poured out of the capital city of Jerusalem into the towns and villages of Judea and Galilee. The church in Jerusalem, at least temporarily, disappeared.

Just as suddenly as was the exodus, came also a whole new generation of churches. Church life as known in the living rooms of Jerusalem now sprang up in living rooms in villages and towns all over Israel.

Even more amazing, out of nowhere sprang a whole new generation of *workers*! The third wave had begun. It had begun in the experience of church life. It had begun as a new breed of workers emerged.

You know them: Philip, Agabus, Silas, Justus and Barnabas. Stephen had been martyred by now.

(There were surely others, but we do not know their names, just as we did not know the names of the seventy who went out in twos in Galilee.)

Note this unusual fact: These churches were not so much planted as they were transplanted. Believers fleeing Jerusalem *all* knew church life. These new churches springing up were simply the church in Jerusalem reconvening in homes all over Israel.

Church members who had experienced church life poured out of Jerusalem by the thousands. Now gathered in other towns, these believers were cut off from the twelve. After six years, God's people were on their own, leaderless. (If you think these churches had elders for leaders, consider this: Even the church in Jerusalem did not have elders. Elders would not appear in the Jerusalem church until fourteen years after Pentecost.) Will the pattern hold out there in Jerusalem? Will God's way of doing things change? Will the pattern hold on all three fronts: Christian life, church life, and for some, workers?

Let us look at the men whom the Lord called out from among the thousands pouring out of the capitol—the men who will be the third generation of workers. Look at these men as: (1) believers living out the Christian life, (2) church members, (3) workers.

The people fleeing into Judea had not known Christ when He was present on earth physically. They all knew Christ, but in a different way than the twelve had known Him. All knew Him *internally*, as the indweller! They learned the "how" of living the Christian life by two means:

(1) *personal* encounter with an indwelling Lord

(2) *corporate* encounters with Christ.

Now, who taught them such wonders? Twelve men, church planters! In the context of the daily life of the ecclesia, people had learned Christ.

Welcome to the Galilean-Judean-Israeli-Syrian experience! They are all the same.

Overnight, around twenty thousand believers were transplanted into the towns and villages of Israel and Syria.

Between fifty and three hundred churches were born as out of thin air, all now within the matrix of God's way of doing things.

This "Jerusalem transplanting" was a unique experience never seen again in the first century. (The birth of the church in Rome was somewhat similar, yet radically different.) In this case, the believers left the church planters, rather than the way it would be in all future situations where the church planters left the believers!

Something else happened which you will note happening again and again in Century One: The believers were left all on their own. Once more the divine principle of the worker abandoning the ecclesia.

There are no leaders. The twelve could not possibly help all these new assemblies on a permanent basis. At best, the twelve would one day visit some of these churches. When the twelve eventually managed to sneak out of Jerusalem, they were able to make infrequent visits to some assemblies. There were simply too many assemblies.

If the twelve went in pairs, that would be a ratio of six men to one hundred ecclesia. Or one pair of church planters for every sixteen churches. You figure it out: How often—and for how long a time—can each church expect to receive help? At best infrequently!

At the time they fled Jerusalem, the brothers, sisters, and the new ecclesias out in Judea were on their own. Actually, that is not exactly true, but they did not really need those twelve men. Six years was enough. They had been *left*, and they were ready. The "Godhead *pattern*" was holding.

Behold, these churches were all operating under the direct

headship of Christ! The invisible Lord was in control, just as He had been when He lived with the twelve.

Just as it is supposed to be. Let Him lead us!

In our age, it is difficult to have a church where Christ alone leads because there are no church planters present at the beginning. (At least no church planters first-century style.)

Your Lord ordained that there be church planters, and those who have tried to have church life without an itinerant church planter have crashed and burned. And those who have had a church planter not of the ancient breed also have crashed and burned, or split, or become a traditional church.

Take a body of people who have been raised up into organic church life and have had a period of help from a church planter. Suppose they have met together, have suffered together, and have been built up together for a long time and then are left alone without a church planter and without leaders. No person in control. No rules or directions or rituals from anyone. If they survive that, and if they continue to exist, and if the church planter comes back and helps them a little periodically and leaves them again. . .then there will be periods of time when the church functions directly under the leadership of Jesus Christ.

But they will always need intermittent visits from the church planter!! That is simply God's way!

Judea—radical! Unprecedented! Unheard of! But still it is God's way!

Church life had taken a step forward because of the events in Judea. God's people in small towns and villages were beholding their Lord. Christ was the center of their ecclesias. There were no dominant leaders in these new churches. Only survivors. All the help they had received in Jerusalem paid off. May all churches have this joyful, scary experience. May you have this experience!

What were the meetings in Judea like? Not too unlike the fellowship and intimacy of Christ and the twelve. Informal. In living rooms. Just like Galilee. Just like Jerusalem.

The Christian life, church life, church meetings were all flowing forth in the pattern. The church was expressed in an organic pattern.

Furthermore, there were some very interesting young men sitting in some of those living rooms. Not one of these young men ever saw Jesus, but they saw Him exhibited by the twelve. And they knew how to live the Christian life after the *Jesus pattern*. And they knew church life as it was known in eternity, in a carpenter shop in Galilee, and in the ecclesia in Jerusalem.

Let's look at these new, sprouting workers a little more closely.

17

If you watched these five young men, you would think for sure that they had physically lived with Jesus. They proclaimed Christ. They so ministered Christ you knew that they had known Him!

These five men—Philip, Barnabas, Agabus, Justus, Silas—had learned how to live the Christian life from the twelve, by means similar to the way the twelve knew Christ. (The twelve in turn had learned from Christ in a way similar to the way Christ had learned church life from the Father.)

These young firebrands, this third generation of Christian workers, embraced that corporate life that they had *in the* church.

All those new workers had lived in the church, getting to know Christ personally and corporately, *long* before they became workers!

Are you called of God? Then take the hint:

First, Christ!

Then the twelve!

Then all that you have read about the third generation of Christian workers!

Learning Christ in church life must/should precede Christian service. And training comes from sitting at the feet of "old" church planters.

What did this third group of young workers learn in the ecclesia? They had grown up in one of the greatest churches in history.* It is important that all knew, therefore, how a new church begins. They knew church life *from the beginning.* No theory. . .no reasoning. . .no speculation. By experience! They could tell you how a church looked when it was new. They *knew* how a new church began.

By having been in church life, what had they learned?

As the twelve had learned the frailties of man back there in Galilee (watching the other eleven make clowns of themselves), these emerging new workers also had learned that same lesson. (How? By watching the other two thousand nine hundred ninety-nine professional sinners, psychotics, liars, thieves, etc, with whom they had been thrown together. And each of these five men, after many failures, eventually had to face the fact that he, too, was a clown.)

These emerging new workers had not seen Jesus minister in Galilee. Before the dispersion, however, when they were in the Jerusalem church, they had watched the men whom Jesus *sent. They*, all five, like thousands after them, met in homes, in an atmosphere not unlike those informal living room meetings in Jerusalem and before that in Galilee with Jesus. They had seen Ananias and Sapphira cheat on living in common. They never forgot that! (Each probably wondered in his own heart why he, too, had not been struck dead.)

What these young men heard, saw, and experienced during those six years in Jerusalem, and in the following years in the

Great churches of Century One were Antioch, Ephesus, and Rome.

small towns of Judea, was *almost* a duplicate of what the twelve had heard and seen and experienced during their years with Jesus.

The pattern. God's way rolls on!

They had seen what the twelve had to pan through and put up with. The twelve had pretty much seen the same when they were with Jesus.

The twelve had been in embryo church life when they saw Jesus carry the burden of ministry. Now these new workers had been right in the middle of church life when they watched the twelve bear the burden of ministry.

This same heritage is what we so desperately need!

If ecclesia life in the church in Jerusalem was anything like church life that spilled out of Jerusalem into Judea and later from there into Antioch. . .and if church life in Antioch was like Galatia, Asia Minor and Europe. . .then you can be sure that everyone's church experience was informal, without ritual, and wholly organic.

If church life is real, be sure it reveals to every man just what a failing Christian he is. All those young men had failed many times, had cried a lot, had often almost given up. Just as the twelve had done! Frequently they had been humiliated in the presence of one another. Just as the twelve had been!

Thank God! May their tribe increase! Without men like these we are never going to get anywhere! Indeed, we will but do what we are doing now—and have for 1700 years— we will sit, profoundly discussing the dandruff that is on our real problems.

We need workers who have grown up in church life thoroughly—men exposed to failure in almost every way possible. It is such men as that who will be tender and patient with God's people. Others will not.

We need men who have experienced in their own lives and the lives of their closest associates the horrendous, fathomless depths of the fall.

Like the twelve, these new workers were professional failures. Like the twelve, they knew one another's worst faults. Like the twelve, they reached the point where no one expected much from anybody. May such men walk this earth again!

Each man could easily, confidently, bring his own sins, weaknesses and problems into the light. All the other men knew the list of faults anyway. There was no need to try to hide something, as he would be greeted with understanding and compassion. Each man was aware that the *others* knew his weaknesses. None of the five was apt to roll over in a dead faint if he had to come dragging some inward flaw into the light.

Each of us should have the right to discover how miserable, conniving, weak, corrupt, and controlling we are. This discovery should and must be made in the context of church life. All men find that out in church life. Such matters cannot be hidden. Your weaknesses are found out. Take heart, everyone else has been found out. In true church life, dozens of Christians *really* know you. You are found out in the holiest place on earth—the church!

You will never find out these things anywhere else. Certainly not by reporting into a building every Sunday morning for an hour!

We have half a million ministers running around on this earth thinking that Christians are capable of living the Christian life. Only in ecclesia life do you find out the *truth*: You cannot!

We have workers working for the Lord who have no long-term experience in body life. (If body life is not an adequate term, let me use the term Christian community.) A worker needs to live for a good length of time in a community of believers in which he is *not* the leader. We have men planting churches who have never known church life. We have men planting house churches who were never previously ordinary brothers in a house church. I would, therefore, say we have many church-life-less workers. .

A church-life-less Christian worker cannot really work effectively with equals, no matter how hard he tries. The mastery of this very difficult art comes about only in real ecclesia life. There are things in our lives that need to be dealt with which only ecclesia life can show us. This is especially true for men who would dare to be Christian workers.

Most church-life-less men do not and cannot know the Lord deeply. Why? Because the experience of knowing an indwelling Christ takes time. So also his training . . .it takes corporateness. This is the norm in church life. What an incubator for young men desiring to be workers!

The church is God's ordained matrix in which you are to experience the cross and brokenness. Anywhere else, your dark side does not come to light as it ought. And a myriad of other things do not find their proper order in the Christian universe either.

Worst of all, a non-church-life worker will almost never be able to raise up a church that is a high and glorious expression of God's eternal purpose. You cannot produce what you have never experienced. When considering a church-life-less worker seeking to build spiritual life in a context outside the traditional church, the phrase "loose cannon on the deck" comes to mind.

Such men also find it hard to live up to the art of departing after having spent a period of time with a church. And if they dare to do so, it meets with disastrous results because people are not prepared well.

Dear reader, we have too many theoreticians running around out there thinking they have figured out what church life is, while sitting in an armchair. They similarly conclude it is not necessary to experience church life before planting church life. Like so much else we receive, what they have to offer is theoretical. Woe to him who follows this piper. My advice? When you hear such wisdom, head for the door!

It is a proud man—an unbroken man—who will not first yield to simply being a brother in the ecclesia before he is a planter of the ecclesia.

Not so with the third generation of first-century workers.

By the time the six years were up and the Jerusalem church was scattered, these new workers had gone through just about everything that the twelve had previously gone through. These young workers now stood in an eternal lineage: the lineage of the "how" of Christian life, the corporate experience of ecclesia life, and sitting at the feet of church planters.

Do not forget it was church planters who trained these young men.

A word to all believers concerning this fellow who wants to help you have church life and who speaks such marvellous words about Scripture: Beautiful words and awesome stories do not a church planter make. Has he paid his dues? For better or worse, has he been in church life? For better or worse, was he trained by a church planter? (A church planter who *departs*? One who *departs* without being pushed out or leaving because he doesn't know what else to do, being out of soap!) Either by design (as Paul and as Jesus) or by osmosis (as the twelve trained the five) was this man trained in his professed calling to be a church planter? If not? You figure it out. . .

The training these young men received was:

(1) in the context of the church,

(2) at the feet of church planters, the only place God ever intended for men and women to be trained as workers.

It is God's way of doing things.

This is more than a method! Much more! This is a divine thing, organic to the nature of God. To raise up workers contrary to this divine organicness is to go at everything the wrong way. This pattern is fundamental to "God's own DNA." It is foundational. The pattern is written into the very bloodstream of the spirituals.

This pattern of all patterns needs to be restored. Now!

We will now leave these young men as they scatter out into the Jewish world. We must now face the vast chasm which separates these Jewish believers from the uncircumcised, unwashed, unclean, heathen Gentiles out there in the future.

Not one of the churches mentioned so far—all of them proceeding out of the loins of Jerusalem—has a single uncircumcised Gentile among them. Something cataclysmic must happen to bring Gentiles into ecclesia life. Something inordinate must happen if this world is to see a church made up of unclean, uncircumcised, unwashed heathen.

Will there be Gentile churches? Will those churches compare with the embryonic church life we have seen in Galilee? Will we see ecclesia life such as that which existed in Jerusalem? Dare we believe those Gentiles will have a relationship with Christ as intimate and personal as did the twelve and the Jerusalem Christians and the transplanted Judean believers? Dare we believe the Gentiles might even have church life that is better than anything the Hebrew believers experienced?

Dare we believe that some of those heathen Gentile

Christians might one day *even* become *workers*? Perish the thought! Such an idea is appalling. Gentile church planters? If such a scandalous thing happens, will those uncircumcised workers be called, raised up, and prepared? In the same way Jesus trained twelve men? And the same way a generation of Jewish workers who never knew Jesus while He was on this earth were raised up?

And will those Gentile workers be sent by the very churches where they had been incubated and raised?

Will the pattern hold?

If so, we present-day Christians with our present evangelical mind-set are in big trouble trying to justify our present-day ways. If the pattern holds, we are obviously looking at nothing less than God's supreme ways.

18

How did the *Gentile story* begin?

A small group of Christians dispersed from Judea made a very big mistake. They entered a northern coastal Syrian city called Antioch. This city was thoroughly Gentile. They hit town preaching like gangbusters! Multitudes responded, but it was the wrong multitude, the wrong race and the wrong culture, with the wrong traditions.

There was hardly a Jewish convert in sight! Look at them—wall to wall heathen! *Heathen* Christians! There is no such thing as heathen . . .pagan. . .infidel. . .*Christians*! Or so it was believed.

Not knowing if they should graduate their converts into church life, these overzealous Jewish men sent a distress signal to Jerusalem.

"Send one of the twelve church planters up here. Fast!"

Ah, but it was not an apostle who alighted from the noon caravan that day. It was Barnabas, *the first to clearly emerge of the third-generation workers.* A new line of

Christian workers was about to be born! Barnabas was about to become a church planter.

Green! Inexperienced! Untested! That was Barnabas— not at all of the stature of the twelve. But he was as prepared as ever a *third motion* worker could be. (Who knows, probably even Barnabas was not aware that he would become one of the greatest church planters of all time.)

Barnabas took one look at the situation in Antioch and quickly decided that there *should be* a heathen, unclean, unwashed, uncircumcised, *Gentile* church on this planet! (How lucky can a people be when getting a church planter? None ever luckier than Antioch!)

That decision took more gall than any other single act found in the first-century church. Barnabas, we who are Gentile are forever in your debt.

When Barnabas saw Antioch, he scratched his head, got a fabulous idea, and grabbed the first camel bound for Tarsus. There he conscripted a Jewish Christian who had grown up among heathen. . .a crusty, highly-educated, trilingual gentleman who, since his conversion, had felt at home with any race, color, tongue, nation, custom, culture or religion. He even claimed that the Lord told him to take Christ to the unclean heathen.

This man's name was Paul.

A New but Controversial Church Planter

Paul would live out his entire life not fully trusted by the Jewish workers and churches who had come before him.

The Jewish workers and Jewish Christians did not believe Paul quite fell into the pattern of God's way of doing things. So, did God bend His pattern just a little? Let us see. . .

Paul returned to Antioch with Barnabas. Paul became a

functioning member of the church in Antioch for the next *four years*.

Yes, Paul became an ordinary brother in church life for four years. Paul also lived daily in the presence of men who had known church life—men who were in the lineage of God's way of doing things. He lived with men who had lived in ecclesia life for seven or more years, men who had experienced church life in Jerusalem and in the towns and cities of Judea. Men who had *been there from the beginning* of church life. The Jerusalem-experienced eyes of Barnabas and others watched Paul every minute of those four years in Antioch.

Paul was observed by some of the most discerning, insightful, spiritual men ever to live on this planet—no less than a group of Jewish prophets and teachers who had come from the original church in Jerusalem. Men who had sat at the feet of the twelve, who, in turn, had sat at the feet of Jesus Christ. They were men who knew how to live the Christian life the way Jesus lived it. They knew the Jesus kind of *church life*, the Apostles kind of church life. All these men had sat at the feet of men trained by Jesus Christ to be church planters.

May you be so blessed! Go! Find such men.

Paul could possibly have fooled you or me or the simple Gentiles of Antioch about his call, his weaknesses, his strengths, his personal life, his hidden motives. But he could not fool *these* men. By the end of those four years, those Jerusalem-experienced brothers knew Paul through and through. His strengths and weaknesses. And loved him anyway. They even liked what they saw! These Jerusalem-trained, Jerusalem-experienced eyes came to trust Paul. They eventually came to trust him as much as they did Barnabas! It was a trust born out of firsthand, prolonged, scrutinizing observation *in the church*!!

Let him who claims to be a church planter offer such credentials to you. Let this be the background of all Christians and all men who dare serve the Lord. Let it be so with you, too, if you aspire to serve the Lord.

Modern-day Christian workers need to pass such a test.

The pattern holds! Even in the Gentile world, even as we approach the possibility of a fourth generation of Christians and workers.

What kind of church life was Paul exposed to?

Gentilish church life. It was church life even more informal than that found in the Jerusalem church or the transplanted Judean churches.

Who raised up this incredible Gentile church? Mostly Barnabas. And pause and remember Barnabas' background and his credentials. And remember: *Paul watched.*

A Look at One of The Third-Generation Workers

Barnabas was saved in Jerusalem. *At the beginning*! Barnabas sat at the feet of twelve church planters for six years. Barnabas fled Jerusalem and experienced church life in Judea.

He was probably present at the birth of *at least* one of the new Judean churches. (Later, when it became possible for the Jerusalem church to begin meeting together again, Barnabas returned to Jerusalem.)

Barnabas spent at least the first six years of his Christian life *not* serving the Lord; *then* he served. Have you an approach to the Christian life or to church life, or to training of workers that matches what Barnabas received? Can you top his quality of Christian service? His knowledge of *how to* live the Christian life?

Paul, a Man Born Out of Season

Was Paul part of the third generation of Christian workers? No! He was not! Can he be counted as one of those in a fourth generation of workers? No! In fact, it will be Paul who raises up a fourth generation of workers!

Paul was a bridge. He came after the third generation of workers, all (but Barnabas) raising up Jewish churches. Paul was a Jew who grew up in a heathen land and went to live in a Gentile church in a Gentile city, and experienced Gentile church life.

He lived his Christian life, as Barnabas did, in a *corporate* context. During the first four years of Paul's church life experience, he did *not* enter Christian service. Paul was in the church in Antioch *from the beginning.* Barnabas was his tutor. Never forget this. *The amazing Paul of Tarsus did not serve the Lord when he was a new Christian.* He did not win souls, did not go off with a para-church organization as a summer missionary. Nothing! (Neither should you. . .para-church organizations nothwithstanding.)

Paul watched another man raise up the church, *from the beginning.* That is God's curriculum! But you cannot find this curriculum in any Bible school or seminary on earth. May you find it in your own life!

Paul had the unparalleled privilege of watching a church planter plant a church, from the beginning. Paul experienced church life before he became a church planter. And, yes, Paul was trained by a church planter.

The pattern held! That is, the pattern continued!

In the meantime, would you, dear reader, make a list of *all* the men on earth today who have been raised up *in this* manner.

Paul sat at the feet of a man who had sat at the feet of the twelve, who had sat at the feet of the Son, who had lived in the presence of His Father for eternity plus thirty years.

Paul was trained by a man who was trained by the twelve, who were trained by Christ, who was trained by the Father; and Paul got this training while being "just a brother."

Yes, the pattern is holding!

Paul's preparation as a worker followed the same pattern as those before him. Barnabas, the twelve, Jesus Christ, the Godhead. As they did, he

(1) learned how to live the Christian life,

(2) experienced church life,

(3) was trained as a worker.

Later in his life we will watch Paul raise up workers. He will do it by the *Jesus pattern*. He will raise up men who will be Gentile workers. He will also train those men with a *Gentile* church in a Gentile city. He was the bridge between the two worlds of the Jewish expression of the church and the Gentile expression of the church.

Why do men today not yield to this pattern? Here are a few guesses: They have no deep revelation of Christ and no revelation of the church. (They don't have time to sit in church life; after all, time is short; Jesus is coming back next Tuesday and the world is going to hell.) They don't need church life! Other traits: Pride. Arrogance. An inability to break the present-day evangelical mind set. Lack of interest in seeing it broken. Addiction to preaching to God's people. A very low view of laymen. The inability to see that laymen with less than a year's experience, and with no designated leaders could be left alone themselves to run the church. More reasons: A shallow view of the Christian faith. Addiction to being a minister. Fear of men. Fear of having to work for a living. Fear of not being *paid* for serving Christ. Fear of being exposed—exposed by laymen, of all people! Addiction to being a pious reverend who is "revered" by laymen. Addiction to the entire spectrum of sacerdotalism. Just plain unwilling to sit at another man's feet and to just be a brother. (To name a few.)

If those divine principles remained so immovable in Century One, it is unlikely God has changed His views to suit the traditions of us evangelicals.

Seminaries were an unplanned accident of history. They were thought up on the spur of the moment in Trent in the mid-1500's and were a copy of the philosophy schools of the ancient Greeks. I do not think you can contort them enough to force them to squeeze into the pattern of how God does things.

The *Jesus pattern* and Aristotle's groves of academia are irreconcilable.

We will get nowhere until we return to spiritual depth, to ecclesia life, the return of the itinerant church planter, and the raising up of workers by the *Jesus pattern*. These are matters too crucial to be any longer *overlooked*.

Now, let us look at that incredible *fourth* generation of *Gentile(!)* workers. If the pattern holds, we should probably be wise to close our seminaries and Bible schools. Not to mention changing our present concept (and practice) of ecclesia. Oh yes, and our approach to *how to live* the Christian life.

19

When Paul of Tarsus began to train Gentile workers, specifically Gentile church planters, he was over fifty years of age and he looked a great deal older. He had every right to look old. His eyes were dimming, his hair gray, his craggy face scarred and wrinkled, his body a scarred disaster. Paul had raised up churches in an area of Asia Minor called Galatia, and he had planted churches in Greece.

It was time.

Paul was about to begin training Gentile church planters. His *pattern* would be the same as Jesus'. Let's watch it unfold.

The Pattern Again

The *first* school for training workers had but two people involved. We have already viewed that school. It was the Lord Jesus trained in eternity by the Father, and then again in time.

The *second* such school was the training of the twelve in Galilee and Judea for three years.

The *third* motion took place in a very religious city, Jerusalem. The students were Silas, Barnabas, Stephen, Agabus, Justus and Philip. All these men were Jews. They, like the twelve, would go to the Jews. (Well, Barnabas fudged a little and went to the Gentiles.)

The *fourth* motion?

This new generation of Christians, this new generation of churches, and finally, this fourth generation of workers is crucial, especially if you happen to be a Gentile!

Just how similar was the raising up of the twelve Jewish workers in Galilee to the raising up of now eight Gentile workers in Ephesus?

The Father prepared the Son, the Son prepared the twelve. He prepared them for a period of *three* years. In Ephesus, you will see that Paul prepared eight men, for *five* years, and deliberately so.

There were two men in the first century who, with deliberate forethought, raised up a group of workers. For one, it took eternity plus thirty years of His life to prepare for that task. And for the other man? Let's see.

By the time Paul reached Ephesus, this itinerant church planter had planted about a dozen churches! Before that he had known church life and had been in church life, in Antioch, Syria. Paul had also sat under Barnabas, both as a Christian learning to live the Christian life and as a man later to become a worker.

In Paul's early Christian years there had been a wilderness experience. Out there Paul had been taught by the Lord Himself. Then came that tutorial time he spent under Barnabas. (Never forget the rich experience Barnabas had, which he brought to Paul. Barnabas was one fantastic mentor!) At the same time Paul was sitting under Barnabas, he learned Barnabas' view of how to live the Christian life, a view Barnabas learned from the twelve, who learned from the Son of God the "how to" of living the Christian life.

Remember Paul was also in the church in Antioch *from the beginning.* Paul spent four years as a member of the body in Antioch. This is the one element in every man's life which never changed: ecclesia life *before* becoming a worker. It ought to be prerequisite in our day. It was there in the ecclesia of Antioch that Paul learned the corporate side of how to live the Christian life.

Later, as a church planter, Paul was shipwrecked, beaten, stoned, mobbed, lied about, written against, damned and criticized. He showed unbelievable grace in the midst of those tragedies and persecutions. Some of that grace he learned from Barnabas. . .who learned it from the twelve. . .who learned it. . .!

The problems Paul faced in those dozen churches he had raised up had almost killed him. Paul, by now, had a built-in broken heart.

Persecuted from one end of the Roman Empire to the other, he was hated and misunderstood by Christians and non-Christians alike. Yet, there he was, old and half blind, still going forward. No bitterness. Scars only on the body, none in heart or soul.

There had been enough problems, crises, failures and injustices in Paul's life to discourage, break, and wreck a dozen Christian workers. But there he is, marching into Ephesus, willing to take on not only lions in Ephesus, but even *eight single brothers*! Wow!

Among mortal men, God's way of doing things is about to hit a new high.

Paul walked into Ephesus knowing just about everything Barnabas knew. He also knew everything Silas knew. He had made four trips to Jerusalem, met Peter three times, the Jerusalem church leaders once, and the twelve once.

Paul has to be the greatest (mortal) church planter of all time, so please note his credentials.

Paul had a great deal to give those eight young men. Not as much as Jesus had to give to the twelve, but more to give than any other man on earth who had *not* physically lived with Jesus. Paul set the standard for how young men are to be trained to be Christian workers. Accept no substitutes.

Never *overlook* another important fact! (It is one of the most exciting thoughts in all of Christian history.) The eight men Paul began training also had a great deal to give to one another. In fact, what each man had to give to the other seven was staggering. What a coming together of trainmanship!

The Cross-Pollination of Gentile Workers

Let's focus on those first few months in Ephesus. We know what Paul brings to this time of training, but what do each of these eight men bring? Their contribution is not small. Each man is a treasure within himself. Where did they come from? What got them to Ephesus? What has each man been through as a Christian and what did he pass through as a member of the body of Christ?

(Later on, in the twilight of the first Christian century, we will see these men raise up a fifth generation of church planters.)

All training should begin with men endowed with experiences as rich as these men bring. Each man had his stories to tell about his country, his culture, and the expression of the body of Christ in his city. Each man could tell the other seven men about the unique planting of their particular church. The story each man told the others was totally different from the rest.

In each case, the birth of the church that each man came from was different. Places were different. Some knew Barnabas but not Silas; some knew Silas and not Barnabas. So it was that each man could tell—and hear—incredibly diverse experiences. These eight men came from six different provinces, spoke different tongues, came from different cultures. They made one another rich in the knowledge of the experiences of the others.

Different churches, different cultures, and different languages. Each lacked the knowledge and experience of the other men, and each gained that knowledge and experience.

Eight men taught and eight men learned—from Paul and from one another. Meet the eight men:

Titus: From the church in Antioch, in a country called Syria. He told the other men all he learned from John Mark and Barnabas. He told, as an eye witness, the story of the birth of the Antioch church. He told about meeting the twelve in Jerusalem, and about the Jerusalem council, and all about what Jerusalem looked like.

Timothy: From the church in Lystra, Galatia. He told the other seven about the birth of the Lystra church, *from the beginning*, and about all he learned from Silas. (Silas had been in Jerusalem *at the beginning* of the church there, just as Barnabas had been, sitting at the feet of the twelve.) Timothy told about what it felt like when Paul and Barnabas walked off and left the Lystra church for two years. He told about Jewish circumcizers making an assault on the four churches in Galatia, about receiving the Galatian letter from Paul. He could talk about that letter both from the view of Paul writing it and the Lystra church receiving it.

Timothy also told the other seven about Paul's entire *second journey* . . .because he went with Paul on that entire second journey. Do you realize that a kid from an obscure little town in Galatia could sit on a floor in a living room and tell you about Paul and Silas being beaten in Philippi, being thrown out of Thessalonica, and raising up the church in Berea. Timothy could tell these other seven men about what Athens looked like. And about Paul's first, second and third visit to Corinth. And how he, Timothy, got involved in the crises in Thessalonica and Corinth. He could tell about visiting Luke, and about going to visit the ecclesia in Antioch. Later he could give a first hand view of what it was like to visit Jerusalem and Rome!

Gaius: From the church in Derbe, located in Galatia. He told the other seven about the birth of the Derbe church . . . how that church was planted and raised up, *from the beginning.* And the leaving of Paul and Barnabas—how that felt. And how the church survived the visit of the circumcisers from Jerusalem. And Paul's letter. And the coming of Paul and Silas.

Sopater, of Berea, Greece, had his story to tell. . .European style.

Aristarchus and Secundus, of northern Greece told their story Thessalonian style. All, from *the beginning.* Aristarchus would later be able to tell you about being imprisoned with Paul in Rome.

Later *Tychicus* and *Trophimus,* of Ephesus, in a tiny province called Asia (not to be confused with what we today call Asia), were added to this number. They could tell the others about life in Ephesus, about the towns and villages just outside Ephesus where Paul took those eight men to watch him plant churches.

Tychicus would later be able to tell them about being in Rome with the imprisoned Paul, and about his trip to Philippi, Greece and the church there, as well as his trip to Colossae, Hierapolis and Laodicea in Asia Minor. And what it was like to know the incredible man named Epaphras. . .who had raised up those churches.

Trophimus could tell them of his trip to Jerusalem with Paul, the ensuing riot, Paul's arrest and imprisonment in Caesarea, and being sent to a faraway land called Dalmatia.

It was the greatest cross-pollination of all time.

Let's watch Paul train these men, and see if we can detect a pattern!

PAUL THE MENTOR

Timothy *saw* Paul stoned in Lystra, whipped in Phillipi, run out of town in Thessalonica and Berea. He watched Paul deal with the church in Corinth with its endless problems. Timothy saw love, patience, forbearance and reality in Paul's life, up close. Then Paul trained Timothy in Ephesus. He watched Paul the prisoner living in Rome.

Titus saw Paul going against twelve apostles, Jews, the Jerusalem elders, *and* the Judaizers in Jerusalem. (He had already witnessed Barnabas and Paul raising up the church in Antioch.) Titus was with Paul throughout his entire third journey. He saw the mob in Ephesus, the problems Apollos created in Corinth. He lived with Paul for years in Ephesus. He saw Paul in Rome, Ephesus, Corinth, Antioch, Jerusalem and outer Greece.

Secundus and Aristarchus watched Paul thrown out of Thessalonica. Trophimus saw Paul almost ripped apart by a mob in Jerusalem.

All the men got to *live with* a church planter who lived an extraordinary life, a life full of pressure.

They watched Paul under stress, pressed out of measure, despairing of life, persecuted, hated, lied about, a man suffering the loss of his ministry. A man facing insuperable odds. They lived with a church planter. They got a ringside look at real Christian ministry—in the extreme.

Twelve men had this same peripatetic life with Jesus. You can't get this from a seminary professor. Are you called of God? May you be trained by a church planter. May you have a mentor, first-century style.

20

Each of these eight men not only had his from-the-beginning story to tell the others, but all these men, together, were about to share a new experience of being there from the beginning. In Ephesus, no less!

Six men, with Paul, enter Ephesus. (Two more are added *in* Ephesus, making a total of eight.) In a nutshell, six men enter Ephesus knowing (1) a total of five from-the-beginnings, (2) five distinct cultures—Syria, two provinces in Galatia, two provinces in Europe (and now Ephesus), plus (3) about half a dozen languages and social habits. The six men would eventually make the entire group cosmopolitan!

Each had a different humor, outlook and personality.

Now they walked into Ephesus, twelve eyes all watching Paul raise up the ecclesia in Ephesus. Six men together sharing another from-the-beginning.

And what a beginning Ephesus was!

All watched the great master builder Paul.

There is no other way a church planter should be trained than *this* way!

Watch these six men, later joined by Tychicus and Trophimus, as they enter Ephesus. They put out of business every reason for every seminary and Bible school that ever existed.

All these men will learn, and learn well, to live the Christian life in a way virtually unknown in our age. Each had known the "how" of living the Christian life in the church they came from. They learned the "how" of living the Christian life from Paul who had learned it from Barnabas, who had learned it from the twelve, who had. . .! And now in Ephesus, older and wiser, they were about to get a refresher course from Paul! Each man had known church life for an average of *over* five years.

Can you say that? Remember, theirs was an experience of a kind of church life of which our age knows virtually nothing.

These young men are coming into existence as church-planters-to-be, by means no man in our age has known, not for over a millennium of years.

The pattern!

Let us get it back! Now!

Watch as the Ephesian story unfolds and becomes the setting of an event basically identical to the ways of Jesus Christ in Galilee.

As noted, two more will join their ranks, Tychicus and Trophimus. They, like the other six, will go on to live a life of grand adventure in the Lord's work.

A ninth man will also join their ranks, Epaphras. He is from Colossae, a small town ninety miles east of Ephesus, a town Paul never visited. We have to assume Epaphras was saved in Ephesus and later returned home to Colossae. This was also true of Philemon, a wealthy man from Colossae, probably saved in Ephesus and greatly influenced by Paul. The church Epaphras raised up in Colossae met in Philemon's home.

As to Epaphras, he rose to become one of the truly great men in the first-century saga, almost a second Paul.

That will bring the Gentile Christian workers to *nine*.

Titus - Antioch
Timothy - Lystra
Gaius - Derbe
Sopater - Berea
Aristarchus - Thessalonica
Secundus - Thessalonica
Tychicus - Ephesus
Trophimus - Ephesus
Epaphras - Colossae

Paul dragged these eight men along with him wherever he went, and then, later, sent them to the ends of the Gentile world. They are the men who gave the gospel and the church to the rest of us Gentiles.

But that is not all. There is evidence that before the century closed, there was yet another generation of workers beginning to emerge. Men emerging within the pattern. It appears that these nine men in Ephesus (the fourth generation of workers) were the very men who trained the *fifth* generation of workers.

Just how qualified would these *Ephesian* trainees be, years later, to raise up another new generation of workers?

Let's see.

21

Eight men went out from Ephesus and scattered out across the Roman Empire. They would age. They would raise up churches, they would show men how to live the Christian life, *and* they would train new workers.

What would it be like to sit under one of the eight Gentile church planters? Something incredible, that's what. Would they also raise up a new generation of church planters? Let's look at some of these men again, this time to see if they look like they might be qualified to raise up a fifth generation of church planters. Just how qualified are these men anyway?

Titus: If Titus entered a city and raised up a church, what experience could he draw from?

He knew the twelve! He knew Barnabas, Silas, John Mark and Luke. Not to mention, he knew Paul. Titus visited Jerusalem another time after that. He could tell you all about the city of Jerusalem. He grew up in the church in Antioch, from the beginning. He was on Paul's church planting trip. He helped in handling the crisis in Corinth. He was trained to be a church planter by one Paul of Tarsus. He lived in Ephesus and its environs for four years.

It can be said that Titus knew the secret to the "how" of living the Christian life. Titus knew church life. He had grown up in the Antioch church. He knew church life in the Jewish world first hand. He knew church life in Greece and Asia Minor, first hand. He was part of the birth of the church in Ephesus.

Titus had sat at the feet of and had been trained by a church planter. Oh, and he knew the other eight. I have a notion that Titus came in second to no one when it came to living *and* showing others. Our last view of Titus? He is on his way to the wild area of Dalmatia to plant churches.

I would say that Titus would one day be very well qualified to raise up a fifth generation of church planters.

Timothy: Most all of the above that is true of Titus is also true of Timothy, except he missed out on the Jerusalem council. He played a major role in Paul's first and second church planting journeys.

He also lived with the imprisoned Paul in Rome. In fact, Paul summarizes some of what Timothy knew, experienced and walked in II Timothy 3: 10-14.

I would say that Timothy was very well qualified to raise up churches—according to the pattern. I would also say that there is every indication that both Titus and Timothy did later raise up a fifth generation of church planters.

Tychicus, Trophimus, Aristarchus: As the first-century story draws to an end, Tychicus is being sent from the island of Crete to Ephesus. (He had served so well in a meeting at Philippi, Colossae, Heropolis and Laodicea that he was sent to Crete to relieve Titus on his church planting ministry to that island.)

Trophimus is still planting churches and is sick in Miletus.

Aristarchus was the first of the eight to die a martyr's death.

We don't know who Artemas is, but it sure looks like we have a *fifth* generation of church planters emerging. (Titus 3:12)

Zenas may also have been part of that next generation of workers. (Titus 3:13)

Do you doubt that these men could match a Paul, a Barnabas, a Peter, a John in showing God's people how Jesus Christ lived the Christian life? Do you think they fell behind in knowing and showing the "how" to the holy ones in the Gentile churches they raised up? Do you doubt they knew church life?

These experiences of church life were so varied and so rich, cutting across so many countries, so many customs, cultures and languages, they may well have known church life better than anyone else who lived in Christian Century One.

If names like Onesiphorus, Erastus, Crescens, Artemas and Zenas are what they very much appear to be, we see these men not only raised up to be workers in the rich legacy of Jesus, the twelve, Barnabas, Silas, Paul and themselves; but as the curtain closes on Century One we may be seeing these Gentile church planters also training a fifth generation of *church planters*. . .by the pattern! By the *Jesus pattern*. By the way God does things—by ways utterly *overlooked* by us.

An incredible saga. A legacy left for us to emulate. An odyssey to replicate.

We need a generation of men as trained and as qualified as these men were, to raise up churches first-century style.

Can such things be restored?

22

To Restore the Pattern

How shall this drama, this *first-century* way, this *divine pattern*, be brought back? Bringing back these ancient ways is difficult, maybe impossible. But let us get caught trying!

In order to restore the pattern, some young men and women who know beyond all doubt that they are called of God to be workers *are going to have to sit down and experience church life!* They are going to have to get to know Christ, and to know *His* way of living the Christian life.

You think finding such hearts will be easy?

Most Christian workers will *not* stop their ministry, will not sit down and become an ordinary brother in the church. . .not for anything! Each man has some great, overriding reason not to do such things. Men have schools to attend, visions to chase, and security to be guaranteed. Further, just stepping out of the mainstream of the evangelical world is as scary as it gets. Try finding such *willing* souls.

More to the point. Find that deep spirit of

humility—humility enough to learn to just be a brother in the ecclesia *first*. . .before *all* else. Try to find one who is *called*, who is willing to simply sit down and be a layman. *Who can find such a man?*

Many look. Many consider. Many ask questions. But exotically rare is the man who dares to stay awhile in church life. Among those, some simply cannot stand the close-up exposure. And that exposure is *very* real.

Are you one who can? And will? Actually men who drop the ministry and start again at *square one* do so only by revelation.

Let us hope that some men will. And then learn the Godhead way of living the Christian life. Learn the organic way of discovering church life. Those who survive? May they be trained and raised up by a church planter—raised up the Galilean way and the Ephesian way.

May all such men put God's people, not ministry, first. May they learn to trust God's people to lead the church *without* their presence. That is, may they get up and leave the churches they raise up. May they be itinerant.

But there is another way that such a new breed of workers can be raised up.

I speak of the possibility that ordinary brothers in the ecclesia—plumbers, mechanics, cooks, computer operators, warehouse workers, sun-crowned men (laymen who were *never* clergy!)—grow up to be Christian workers. To organically rise up out of *the ecclesia* and become trained in that long-lost *first-century style* of becoming workers.

God, haste *that* day.

Yes, this is hopelessly impossible, but the cause worth dying for is a hopeless cause. *This* is a hopeless cause.

* * *

I have written so that God's people who are in a living experience of body life will understand what is going on in their midst, should such men appear. This book is also written to be a lighthouse to young men called of God, in the hope it will light their way to their true call, their organic home, their natural habitat, and to bring them to see that the place intended for them to receive their God-ordained preparation is there, in just such a church.

The untold story of what happened in Ephesus, Paul bringing eight men from diverse churches, is, for me, the most incredible story found in all the first-century records of the ecclesia. This story needs desperately to be known, and then to be re-experienced in your day.

I hope to live long enough to publish a *companion book to *Overlooked Christianity* that centers on *how* the Lord Jesus and Paul raised up workers.

Let us all hope that there will be an Ephesus experience of the raising up of workers in *your* lifetime. God give, in your days, a handful of church planters, first-century style. Perhaps from that seedbed, our earth will see again the "how" to live the Christian life as it ought to be—*and* church life as it is supposed to be. And workers as they are intended to incubate . . .workers raised up as they are supposed to be raised up.

A return to *the ways of the Godhead* in your lifetime.

And now, Spirit of God, find, touch and humble those young men called of God. Place them in ecclesia life and restore *the pattern*!!

And *you*? Make a beeline for church life.

In the companion book of this volume, we will look deeper into Jesus' way and Paul's way. We will cover the practical side of: (1) how to live the Christian life. (2) How to experience the life of the ecclesia. (3) How workers can be trained up in Jesus' way or Paul's way.

23

I belong to the part of *the house church movement* that has small groups in whose gatherings there is no one in charge. Elders come later on, and usually are unrecognizable except in a crisis. This quest to return to a more primitive experience of the faith appears to be a truly spontaneous phenomenon; however, I see in the house church movement at large what I believe to be serious flaws.

What flaws? Most men leading this movement have *never* even remotely experienced anything similar to organic church life. They are theorists. . .working by theory. They are out there trying to sew together something that they refer to as a *New Testament church.* (It is a church that is more made out of verses than out of divine encounter.) These are men who did not grow up in, or live in, church life. In those churches there is still the residue of clergy/laymen. ("I preach, you listen.")

There is a great deal of talk about all sorts of things in the house church movement, but very little of it is Christ. There is little indication that what happens is coming from a deep revelation of Christ, followed by a deep experience of Christ. Little is said about the ecclesia, little is known of the ecclesia, little is experienced of the ecclesia, even though this is a movement intent on returning to the ecclesia. That is, little that is said reflects a deep revelation of the church.

There is also little said about restoring church planters. The idea that the incubator and habitat from which church planters are supposed to be born is church life and only church life, is considered a "turn off." It is a turn-off conversation when the subject comes up that workers should be itinerant. Much is said about ethics, discipline, administration, gifts and prophecy, but virtually nothing of the singular need of men to be called, trained, and sent as church planters, first-century style.

All Christian workers are supposed to be trained by church planters. All workers today should be trained on the foundation of the Ephesus pattern; for this is, and always will be, God's way of doing things in the age of the ecclesia. The first century gives us no other way.

(And you want to go to Bible school? Remember, institutions such as seminaries are totally without scriptural justification. Men raised up by church planters, folks, and only by church planters! Itinerant church planters!)

The pattern is always the same.

Is it not, therefore, extraordinary that this pattern is not followed in Christianity today?

There is one New Testament aspect of church planting I find *no* Christian workers to be interested in. That is, that early on in the life of every new church, the church planter gets up and departs that church. He does so at a time not too far distant from the birth of that church. . .at a time when there is a leave-her-on-her-own, sink-or-swim situation. He also departs from that ecclesia. . .*without* its having elders or leaders present. I have never witnessed a serious admission that there is such a concept in the New Testament—even though this is *Paul's consistent* pattern. Nobody seems to even breathe in the direction of shaping his life in so dramatic a way.

If we do not first experience church life before planting churches, we are nothing but theorists. We have nothing to give.

If we who dare plant a church. . .if we do not walk out on the church, leaving her to develop her own personality, her own organic expression, one native to her matrix and culture (if we stay in the ecclesia we raise up), then we will *never* see organic church life on this planet.

Not possible? Paul did it every time. He had an eighteen-month limit on staying in a church. And a few other men in later times have dared. The results were incomparably beautiful.

But here is the one overlooked aspect which troubles me the most. I see little interest in *spiritual depth* among those who are planting churches. (I am not talking about "pray, fast, read your Bible.") I don't see any clues that a deep, profound walk with Christ in realms invisible is of central importance. Dare we say that most men do not even show interest or know what is being discussed when it is brought up!

Little discernible interest in the deeper things of Christ. Not time enough to drop everything, lay down everything and get to know the Lord Jesus *very* well! Once more, the center of one's faith *overlooked!*

Virtually never does anyone minister on these subjects. Where is that desperate cry, "Show me, at any cost," which wells up out of broken men who see that they do not know the Lord very well, and the cross not at all.

My deepest impression is that most men in the ministry do not know there is the possibility of a deep and consistent encounter with Christ. Furthermore, my impression is that men do not believe there is such a thing. I dare to believe that this is the simple truthful explanation—men just don't know such a walk exists. I have to believe this is the reason. Otherwise, we would be facing an even worse explanation: not only that men do not believe there is a deeper walk with Christ, but that they are not interested in getting to know Christ and His cross in an intimate way.

All this should be the repertoire of all men who dare to train men to be church planters. And for those who would even dare to think about raising up a new generation of church planters? Add a *lifetime* of church planting!

May God send a desperate hunger to men called of God *to want to know their Lord deeply.* To know how to encounter Him, deeply. Again, I speak not of Bible study, nor prayer, nor tongues. I speak of things that are inexplicable: realms unseen and things invisible.

May God also send this hunger to the simple, ordinary, everyday layman. To *know* Him. And to be in the life and the experience of the ecclesia.

The ecclesia, after all, is exactly the source from which God drew Christian workers in Century One.

Do it again, Lord.

24

A Closing Word

I wrote the first draft of this book when I was thirty years old. That was half a lifetime ago.

I waited thirty-four years to release this book. But I also waited this long to begin training men.

Only recently I gathered a small group of men and lived with them for an extended period of time, training them to one day be workers. These men were all laymen. They *grew up* in ecclesia life. They were selected from out of their respective churches. (God pity those men if they ever try to go home and begin acting important, because they each came out of a strong brotherhood. A *very* strong brotherhood.)

Not all these men will become workers. Perhaps one or two will eventually become planters of ecclesias. That is not the point. The point is, here are resemblings of the ancient ways! There will be new church life; and, if God so wills that a few more men are in a few more times of training, then there will be workers first-century style. Men who grew up in the ecclesia. . .to receive training to work. The thought is terrifying—a new breed of workers, raised up in a wholly new, revolutionary way.

It is my hope that I have given those men Christ, by the ancient ways. It is my belief that they have experienced ecclesia life, first-century style. I trust that their training bears some of the marks of those ancient ways which we saw in the first century and which had their origins in heavenly places, before creation.

I hope other men in other places and in other nations will abandon the evangelical mind-set, and take up *this* banner, to come back to ways which belong to the eternals.

Then, maybe, just maybe. . .

OTHER THINGS
WE HAVE OVERLOOKED

OVERLOOKED
CHURCH HISTORY

Here are some footnotes from church history you are not likely to find in any traditional history book. As you read, consider the evangelical mind-set. All the following facts tell you where we got those evangelical practices which we hold to be sacred. None of them are remotely scriptural and none reflect anything of the ecclesia of Century One.

While you read, listen carefully and you may hear the not-so-distant voice of an evangelical pastor or a fundamental theologian crying out, "We must be faithful to the Word of God!" When you finish reading this list of practices and see the time frame in which they appeared in history, ask yourself just how scriptural our evangelical Christianity is.

* * *

Pastors are an invention of the Reformation. Nothing remotely similar to them existed in the first century.

*Elders are mentioned in the New Testament seventeen times. *Pastor* one time! And that first-century man has no equivalent

---

* *See* **Rethinking Elders,** *available from The SeedSowers Publishing House.*

in our present-day practice.

Brothers and *sisters,* on the other hand, are mentioned over 130 times!

Who is in charge in the church? Who is at center stage? The fellow mentioned once? The men mentioned seventeen times? Or those who crowd the action taking place in the first-century story? That is: the brothers and sisters. . .over 130 times!

Seminaries began in 1540 . . . coming out of the Catholic Council of Trent. Those first seminaries were based on a curriculum that emerged in the darkest days of the Dark Ages. *Protestant seminaries* and evangelical *Bible schools* are a carbon copy of these academic institutions of learning which bear absolutely *no* similarity to the way Christian workers were raised up in Century One.

The Protestant *choir* came from the Catholic choir, which, in turn, evolved from choirs in heathen temples.

Choir *leaders* (song leaders, worship leaders, ministers of music) are a development of recent Protestantism. Note that none of these leaders ever let God's people function in a meeting. They don't even get to start songs in a worship service.

Church buildings began in 327 A.D.; nothing like them existed before that. (All the ecclesia mentioned in the New Testament met in *homes.* Not in church buildings, *ever.* Primitive Christianity was a living room movement.)

Sermons were not invented until 400 A.D. They became the stable fare of Protestantism in the early 1500's.

The practice of *going to a building* every Sunday to hear someone bring a sermon began in about 400 A.D. Going to a church building and hearing the *same* person preach a sermon to you, year in and year out, did not make its appearance until the Reformation. It was a concept introduced by Luther and Calvin.

The *ritual* you follow every Sunday—the Sunday morning *order of worship*—was invented by John Calvin, about 1540.

In Century One everyone started songs, everyone shared, everyone preached and everyone "led."

The idea of *home Bible classes* took root in Great Britain and North America in the 1880's. It may rattle your cage to even think this next thought, but there is no New Testament justification for home Bible classes! In the first century it was the ecclesia, only the ecclesia, and nothing but the ecclesia. All things flowed to the church and from the church.

Eldership as practiced by most house churches was a concept invented out of thin air by John Darby about 1840. This leadership concept and practice has no scriptural grounds whatsoever. (Verses can justify it, but then *verses* can justify anything! The sweeping story of the chronology of Century One, as seen in Scripture, allows no such practice nor concept.)

The invention of the *pew* followed the invention of the church building. First it was a backless stool, about 327 A.D. Then a bench with a back on it, about 1500. Then a modern pew, about 1600. Now the *padded* pew, about 1900.

Stained glass windows? They came about 1200 A.D.

The *interdenominational organization* (now referred to as the para-church organization) was invented about 1880 in the advent of the YMCA and the Student Christian Voluntary Movement. John R. Mott and D. L. Moody invented these, taking their cue from the "Christian orphanage movement" of that era.

This era began the mind-set that allows a man to peer into

the New Testament and find soul winning on virtually every page—and find the ecclesia hardly at all.

The present-day evangelical mind-set, accepting of all of the above, is entrenched so deeply in all of us that it will still be here at the dissolution of creation. In fact, this mind-set has become so much a part of us that we can study the New Testament and find, not first-century practices, but all of the above-mentioned practices! That's some feat! Yet the evangelical Christian mind, and its ability to see in the New Testament things which are not there, blocks any hope of that mind's grasping the real atmosphere of Century One.

In the meantime, the first-century practices are overlooked. This is *Overlooked Christianity*.

What you and I are taught as being practices in the New Testament . . . *ain't*!

We also divided the New Testament into *chapters and sentences*. Then we gave the sentences numbers. Today a chapter-and-verse mentality is a convenient way to hack people to bits if they don't share your views.

The Arrangement of Paul's Letters in the New Testament

Luther arranged Paul's letters, not in the order Paul wrote them, but in Luther's favorite view of their doctrinal content. If you know the chronological order of these letters, then you wonder how Luther ever came up with such a bizarre arrangement. Paul's letters are arranged in this chaotic order— 6th, 4th, 5th, 1st, 8th, 10th, 7th, 2nd, 3rd, 12th, 11th, 13th, 9th— rather than in chronological order as they were written.

If we continue to put out New Testaments with Paul's

books arranged in this madcap order created by Luther, we will *never* catch the sense of what happened among the first-century Christians.

The First-Century Story

Did you know that no book has ever appeared that tells the *entire* story of the first century? In all the millions of books written in Christendom, no one saw the need to place context (the story) *above* chapter and verse!

If that story is ever told, and if you read it, you will find in it no present-day practice of pastors, church buildings, services, inter-denominational organizations, and all the other trappings we take for granted as being part of the early faith. Most of all, you will not find our evangelical mind-set.

You can find anything in verses, but *in the story* you will find nothing of present-day evangelical practices.

What is the story? What is in it? Who really are the central players? This book gives you a glance. Perhaps, one day, the entire story will be told.

In the meantime, God's ways of doing things are not our present ways.

We have looked at the overlooked. Now it is time to overlook what we presently have, and return to God's ways of doing things.

Those ways wait to be restored. God haste the day!

THINGS WE OVERLOOKED
WE DARE NOT LOOK AT

Today's concept of elders would collapse (and should collapse) if we admit that all local elders were ordained by the non-local church planter.

Do you like the book of Acts? Well, that book centers on the story of non-local, trans-local, extra-local, itinerant church planters. We don't have any of these!

Do you like Galatians? It was written to a church—a body of people—*not* to an individual. This book was written by a non-local, itinerant church planter. The primary relevance of Galatians is to an ecclesia. It has no relevance to a believer who is not in a functioning ecclesia that is expressing church life. At least, the author had no such thought in mind when he penned it. This book is for a people experiencing church life.

Do you like I Thessalonians and II Thessalonians? These two books were written to an ecclesia by a man who was a non-local worker who planted that church. The relevance of those two books? See above.

Do you like I Corinthians and II Corinthians? These two books were written to a church, by a non-local, itinerant church planter.

Do you like Romans? How about Colossians, Ephesians and Philippians? See above.

Three books are mis-named *the pastoral epistles*. I Timothy and Titus, and II Timothy. These three books were written by a church planter to two younger church planters. They were never referred to as *the pastoral epistles* until *after* Luther invented the modern day pastor concept.

I Peter and II Peter? They were written by a church planter to the Jewish churches which he, Peter, planted. A book by a church planter to churches. . .never intended by the author to be used in a non-church-life environment.

We wish very much to *overlook* these facts. If we cannot overlook all this, we have to return to the practice of itinerant, non-local church planters. We would also have to give up the modern-day pastoral role.

In fact, we would have to start all over again!

Radical Books for Radical Readers

Overlooked Christianity
Beyond Radical
Rethinking Elders
Revolution
The Silas Diary *(coming in Summer of 1998)*
How To Meet Under The Headship Of Jesus Christ
When The Church Was Led By Laymen
Climb The Highest Mountain

Books on the Deeper Christian Life

The Highest Life
The Secret To The Christian Life
The Inward Journey

Books which Inspire

The Divine Romance
The Chronicles of the Door:
  The Beginning
  The Escape
  The Birth
  The Triumph
  The Return

Books that Heal

Crucified by Christians
The Prisoner in the Third Cell
A Tale of Three Kings

Available from:

The SeedSowers
P.O.Box 285, Sargent, GA 30275
Ph: 1-800-645-2342

**Order From Your Local Bookstore
or SeedSowers Publishing House**

Books by Gene Edwards

Prices at 1997

Overlooked Christianity	14.95
The Silas Diary *(Summer 1998)*	TBA
Beyond Radical	4.00
When the Church was Led Only by Laymen	4.00
An Open Letter To House Church Leaders	4.00
Crucified by Christians	8.95
The Secret To The Christian Life	8.95
The Highest Life	8.95
The Prisoner In The Third Cell	7.95
A Tale Of Three Kings	8.95
How To Meet	11.95
The Divine Romance	8.95
The Inward Journey	8.95
Letters To A Devastated Christian	5.95
Revolution, *The Story Of The Early Church*	8.95
Climb The Highest Mountain	9.95
The Chronicles Of The Door: The Beginning	7.95
The Escape	8.95
The Birth	8.95
The Triumph	8.95
The Return	8.95

Books by Jeanne Guyon

Experiencing The Depths Of Jesus Christ	8.95
Union With God	8.95
Spiritual Torrents	8.95
Guyon Speaks Again	8.95
Final Steps In Christian Maturity	8.95
Song Of The Bride	9.95
Christ Our Revelation	9.95

Great Books By Other Authors

Bone of His Bone *(F.J. Huegel)*... 8.95
The Centrality of Christ *(T.Austin Sparks)*........................... TBA
Christ as All in All *(Haller)*.. 9.95
The Key to Triumphant Living *(Taylor)*................................ 9.95
Which Being Interpreted Means *(Taylor)*............................. 7.95
The Open Church *(Rutz)*.. 8.95
The Seeking Heart *(Fenelon)*... 8.95
Church Unity *(Nee, Litzman, Edwards)*................................. 8.95
Let's Return To Christian Unity *(Kurosaki)*........................... 8.95
You Can Witness With Confidence *(Rinker)*...........................8.95
Turkeys And Eagles *(Peter Lord)*...8.95
Going To Church In The First Century *(Banks)*......................5.95
When The Church Was Young *(Loosley)*.................................7.95
The Passing Of The Torch *(Chen)*...7.95
Practicing His Presence *(Lawrence, Laubach)*........................ 8.95
The Spiritual Guide *(Molinos)*.. 8.95
Torch Of The Testimony *(Kennedy)*.. 9.95
Church Life Before Constantine *(Snyder)*............................ 19.95
Beholding And Becoming *(Coulter)*..8.95

Available from:

The SeedSowers
P.O.Box 285, Sargent, GA 30275
Ph: 1-800-645-2342